More Praise for *Your Church in Rhythm*

"The myth of a perfectly balanced ministry is just that, a myth. Worse, the pursuit of it is a certain recipe for needless frustration and discouragement. Bruce Miller offers an alternative that is true to both Scripture and creation—a powerful force called rhythm."—Larry Osborne, author and pastor, North Coast Church, Vista, California

"*Your Church in Rhythm* will stop you in your tracks and then move you forward in a more healthy way. We all struggle to refine and sustain our leadership. Bruce Miller brings critical insights into seasons inherent in the life and the leadership of the church. Rhythmic understanding can make the difference between success and failure, creative vitality, and resigned mediocrity. *Your Church in Rhythm* will ultimately change the way you lead."—Jim Garlow, lead pastor, Skyline Church, La Mesa, California

"Any pastor who has struggled finding 'balance' will benefit by discovering 'rhythm' instead. Grow past the nonstop hype of making every Sunday 'the greatest Sunday ever!' *Your Church in Rhythm* brings ministry back to reality."—Geoff Surratt, pastor of ministries, Seacoast Church, Mt. Pleasant, South Carolina

"Bruce Miller leads a healthy, growing church because he lives a healthy, ever-growing life that is in step with the Spirit. He has discovered what so many pastors and leaders search for—a Spirit-directed rhythm within the Body that brings forth sustained growth over the long haul. Every pastor and church leader needs to read this book!"—Jeff Warren, senior pastor, Park Cities Baptist Church

"This very practical book will help all pastoral leaders carry out Paul's powerful exhortation—to make 'the most of every opportunity' (Ephesians 5:16)."—Dr. Gene A. Getz, Center for Church Renewal, Plano, Texas

"As a pastor, I'm constantly searching for the best resources to train and equip my staff and church leaders. *Your Church in Rhythm* just moved to the top of my list."—Dr. Chip Henderson, pastor, Pinelake Church, Brandon, Michigan

"In *Your Church in Rhythm*, Bruce Miller unpacks a truth that I believe can not only save a pastor a lot of heartache, but can inject a lot of life into the heart of a church. Recognizing the 'seasons' in the life of our church has been very liberating and energizing for us. My prayer is that you'll find yourself more excited about the present and the future of your church than ever before as you read this book."—Dino Rizzo, lead pastor, Healing Place Church, Baton Rouge, Louisiana

"Mandatory reading for pastors, staff, church leaders, and members for Bruce's rich insight to engaging the rhythms of church life rather than fighting against the rhythms. His description of how God has woven rhythms into the life of every ministry is a priceless principle."—Bryan L. Carter, senior pastor, Concord Church

"One of the signs of a good book is that as you are reading it you want to thank the author for writing it. *Your Church in Rhythm* has been that kind of book for me. This provides a common language from which church leaders can have robust conversation around where their church is at, and what God is calling them to do and not to do. Most of all, *Your Church in Rhythm* invites the reader to establish a new definition of health for themselves, their leaders, and their church. Thank you, Bruce."—Scott Wilson, senior pastor, The Oaks

Bruce B. Miller

Your**Church** in**Rhythm**

Foreword by Will Mancini

JOSSEY-BASS
A Wiley Imprint
www.josseybass.com

A Leadership ❈ Network Publication

Published by Jossey-Bass
A Wiley Imprint
989 Market Street, San Francisco, CA 94103-1741—www.josseybass.com

Readers should be aware that Internet Web sites offered as citations and/or sources for further information may have changed or disappeared between the time this was written and when it is read.

Jossey-Bass books and products are available through most bookstores. To contact Jossey-Bass directly call our Customer Care Department within the U.S. at 800-956-7739, outside the U.S. at 317-572-3986, or fax 317-572-4002.

Scriptures taken from the Holy Bible, New International Version®, NIV®. Copyright © 1973, 1978, 1984 by Biblica, Inc.™ Used by permission of Zondervan. All rights reserved worldwide. www.zondervan.com

Jossey-Bass also publishes its books in a variety of electronic formats. Some content that appears in print may not be available in electronic books.

Library of Congress Cataloging-in-Publication Data
Miller, Bruce B., date
    Your church in rhythm : the forgotten dimensions of seasons and cycles / Bruce B. Miller.
        p. cm. – (Jossey-Bass leadership network series ; 52)
    Includes bibliographical references and index.
    ISBN 978-0-470-59887-0 (hardback); 978-0-470-94721-0 (ebk); 978-0-470-94722-7 (ebk); 978-0-470-94723-4 (ebk)
        1. Church management.   2. Time management–Religious aspects–
Christianity.   3. Time.   4. Time–Religious aspects–Christianity.   I. Title.
    BV652.M555   2011
    254–dc22

                                                                                          2010043459

Printed in the United States of America
FIRST EDITION
HB Printing   10 9 8 7 6 5 4 3 2 1

LEADERSHIP NETWORK TITLES

The Blogging Church: Sharing the Story of Your Church Through Blogs, Brian Bailey and Terry Storch

Church Turned Inside Out: A Guide for Designers, Refiners, and Re-Aligners, Linda Bergquist and Allan Karr

Leading from the Second Chair: Serving Your Church, Fulfilling Your Role, and Realizing Your Dreams, Mike Bonem and Roger Patterson

Hybrid Church: The Fusion of Intimacy and Impact, Dave Browning

The Way of Jesus: A Journey of Freedom for Pilgrims and Wanderers, Jonathan S. Campbell with Jennifer Campbell

Cracking Your Church's Culture Code: Seven Keys to Unleashing Vision and Inspiration, Samuel R. Chand

Leading the Team-Based Church: How Pastors and Church Staffs Can Grow Together into a Powerful Fellowship of Leaders, George Cladis

Organic Church: Growing Faith Where Life Happens, Neil Cole

Church 3.0: Upgrades for the Future of the Church, Neil Cole

Journeys to Significance: Charting a Leadership Course from the Life of Paul, Neil Cole

Off-Road Disciplines: Spiritual Adventures of Missional Leaders, Earl Creps

Reverse Mentoring: How Young Leaders Can Transform the Church and Why We Should Let Them, Earl Creps

Building a Healthy Multi-Ethnic Church: Mandate, Commitments, and Practices of a Diverse Congregation, Mark DeYmaz

Leading Congregational Change Workbook, James H. Furr, Mike Bonem, and Jim Herrington

The Tangible Kingdom: Creating Incarnational Community, Hugh Halter and Matt Smay

Baby Boomers and Beyond: Tapping the Ministry Talents and Passions of Adults over Fifty, Amy Hanson

Leading Congregational Change: A Practical Guide for the Transformational Journey, Jim Herrington, Mike Bonem, and James H. Furr

The Leader's Journey: Accepting the Call to Personal and Congregational Transformation, Jim Herrington, Robert Creech, and Trisha Taylor

Whole Church: Leading from Fragmentation to Engagement, Mel Lawrenz

Culture Shift: Transforming Your Church from the Inside Out, Robert Lewis and Wayne Cordeiro, with Warren Bird

Church Unique: How Missional Leaders Cast Vision, Capture Culture, and Create Movement, Will Mancini

A New Kind of Christian: A Tale of Two Friends on a Spiritual Journey, Brian D. McLaren

The Story We Find Ourselves In: Further Adventures of a New Kind of Christian, Brian D. McLaren

Missional Renaissance: Changing the Scorecard for the Church, Reggie McNeal

Practicing Greatness: 7 Disciplines of Extraordinary Spiritual Leaders, Reggie McNeal

The Present Future: Six Tough Questions for the Church, Reggie McNeal

A Work of Heart: Understanding How God Shapes Spiritual Leaders, Reggie McNeal

The Millennium Matrix: Reclaiming the Past, Reframing the Future of the Church, M. Rex Miller

Your Church in Rhythm: The Forgotten Dimensions of Seasons and Cycles, Bruce B. Miller

Shaped by God's Heart: The Passion and Practices of Missional Churches, Milfred Minatrea

The Missional Leader: Equipping Your Church to Reach a Changing World, Alan J. Roxburgh and Fred Romanuk

Missional Map-Making: Skills for Leading in Times of Transition, Alan J. Roxburgh

Relational Intelligence: How Leaders Can Expand Their Influence Through a New Way of Being Smart, Steve Saccone

Viral Churches: Helping Church Planters Become Movement Makers, Ed Stetzer and Warren Bird

The Externally Focused Quest: Becoming the Best Church for the Community, Eric Swanson and Rick Rusaw

The Ascent of a Leader: How Ordinary Relationships Develop Extraordinary Character and Influence, Bill Thrall, Bruce McNicol, and Ken McElrath

Beyond Megachurch Myths: What We Can Learn from America's Largest Churches, Scott Thumma and Dave Travis

The Other Eighty Percent: Turning Your Church's Spectators into Active Participants, Scott Thumma and Warren Bird

The Elephant in the Boardroom: Speaking the Unspoken About Pastoral Transitions, Carolyn Weese and J. Russell Crabtree

CONTENTS

ABOUT**THE**JOSSEY-BASS LEADERSHIPNETWORK SERIES

L eadership Network's mission is to accelerate the impact of One-HundredX leaders. These high-capacity leaders are like the hundredfold crop that comes from seed planted in good soil as Jesus described in Matthew 13:8.

Leadership Network...

- Explores the "what's next?" of what could be
- Creates "aha!" environments for collaborative discovery
- Works with exceptional "positive deviants"
- Invests in the success of others through generous relationships
- Pursues big impact through measurable Kingdom results
- Strives to model Jesus through all we do

Believing that meaningful conversations and strategic connections can change the world, we seek to help leaders navigate the future by exploring new ideas and finding application for each unique context. Through collaborative meetings and processes, leaders map future possibilities and challenge one another to action that accelerates fruitfulness and effectiveness. Leadership Network shares the learnings and inspiration with others through our books, concept papers, research reports, e-newsletters, podcasts, videos, and online experiences. This in turn generates a ripple effect of new conversations and further influence.

In 1996, Leadership Network established a partnership with Jossey-Bass, a Wiley Imprint, to develop a series of creative books that provide thought leadership to innovators in church ministry. Leadership Network publications present thoroughly researched and innovative concepts from leading thinkers, practitioners, and pioneering churches.

Leadership Network is a division of OneHundredX, a global ministry with initiatives around the world.

To learn more about Leadership Network, go to www.leadnet.org.

To learn more about OneHundredX, go to www.100x.org.

FOREWORD

If genius is the ability to illuminate the obvious, then Bruce Miller is a genius. The insights in this book just might transform how you lead for the rest of your life.

Rhythm is everywhere, in every moment. Your brain cells, this moment, receive life with each heartbeat. In this moment, you are whirling unaware in patterned motion as planet Earth spins like a bike wheel and pedals its orbit around the sun. Inside of you and all around you, reality dances to the cadences of the creator's music. When God painted this world, his favorite brushstroke was rhythm.

Yet we are tempted to miss this fundamental context of our lives. Rhythm to us is like water to a fish. As such, the reality of rhythm becomes something we take for granted. It's always there but rarely explored.

Hence, this book is a wake-up call for every leader who has not yet examined rhythm as a feature of life in general and church life in particular. I know I've been guilty. The alarm clock's ring left a powerful question—both challenging and haunting—echoing in my mind: "What if, in our casual awareness of rhythm's ever-present dynamic, we have missed the deepest wisdom of leadership?"

Prepare for this book to sound the perils of ignoring rhythm. Guilt, busyness, stress, and even despair can win the day in our "rhythm-dumb" approaches. Among many strategies stained with artificial idealism, Bruce Miller debunks the kingpin—the notion of "balance" that marks many of our mental models in ministry.

As you dive into this book, I am particularly excited to commend three other aspects:

First, the principles of this book are incredibly actionable. Bruce boils down six simple and compelling strategies that you can take and use everywhere you go. Don't be surprised when you get up from your favorite reading nook to find these six new tools strapped to your pastoral tool belt.

Second, the principles of this book are universally applicable. There is no time or place and there is no theological conviction or leadership style where rhythm doesn't apply. If you, like me, are tired of the myriad of "how-to-do-church" books, then be happy! *Your Church in Rhythm* delivers 24-karat gold by transcending models, methods, and trends.

Third, the author of this book is a one-of-a-kind Kingdom laborer. As a leader, Bruce couples the mind of a military strategist with the heart of a willing foot soldier. As a follower of Jesus, he fuses intensity with integrity and honesty with optimism like no one I know. Over the last twelve months, I have enjoyed getting to know Bruce and his team. They glow with a rare spirit that is *"All in"* and *"All together"* for Jesus.

Now, with the turn of each page, journey into this lost river of wisdom. From wet feet to waist deep, you will discover that which is at once strangely familiar and yet completely new.

Will Mancini
Founder, Auxano, and author, *Church Unique*

PREFACE

It was July in Aukland, New Zealand, at a leadership conference, when it first struck me that the idea of a so-called balanced life is unbiblical, impossible, and toxic. Instead, rhythm offers a much richer picture of a healthy life. My earlier book *Your Life in Rhythm* paints that picture of a rhythmic life.

Two friends, Mark Sweeny and Greg Ligon, asked me if "rhythm" could apply to churches. If a rhythmic life is better than a balanced life, would not a rhythmic church be better than a balanced church? It made sense to me. If living life in rhythm leads to less stress and more fulfillment, could it be that doing church in rhythm would also reduce unnecessary stress while increasing effectiveness? These questions took me on a journey that eventually led to *Your Church in Rhythm*.

Along the way our church contracted with Will Mancini and the Auxano organization to consult with us. As the author of *Church Unique*, Will has an amazing ability to help leaders clarify the unique identity of their organization. When Will and I discussed uniqueness and rhythm, we recognized that both rhythm and uniqueness are "metaconcepts." Metaconcepts are unbounded by the size, age, or theology of a local church. A metaconcept transcends most categories that divide and distinguish churches.

No matter what strategy, model, or approach you take, identity and timing are relevant to your ministry. No matter what its culture, structure, or style, a local church carries out its mission in rhythmic seasons and cycles. To be effective for Christ and for ministry to be truly enjoyable, churches need to know what time it is. In what unique time is your church ministering? I've written this metaconcept book for church leaders of all flavors in the hope that it will contribute to making your ministry more effective and enjoyable.

In the following chapters, we will peer into the forgotten dimension of time and explore two kinds of rhythm: chronos and kairos. You and your fellow leaders will learn how to discern "what time it is in your church" by identifying your organizational stage and ministry seasons. When you grasp your "time," you can apply the kairos rhythm strategies to focus on what will most advance Christ's mission in this unique moment for your church. When you recognize the five chronos cycles embedded in our natural world, the three chronos rhythm strategies will empower you to pace your church, build mission-enhancing rituals, and oscillate intensity and renewal so that you prevail for a lifetime in fruitful ministry. My hope is to open your eyes to a new horizon that offers fresh insights to strengthen your church's ministry and lighten your burden as you serve Christ.

ACKNOWLEDGMENTS

I thank God for Jennie Tissing, who aided me in preparing the manuscript and kept step with me in the intense times. Laurie Wright, my excellent assistant, maintained faithful support and kept all communication on track. Most of all, I thank God for my wife, Tamara, without whom I would be lost and this book would not exist. All glory to the King of Kings.

INTRODUCTION

Time:TheForgotten Dimension

We want our churches to be effective for Jesus Christ. And yet, we're not satisfied with what's happening. Not enough people are coming to Christ. Average church members are not serious enough about their faith. There is no silver bullet, no one solution. But there is a dimension many church leaders have not adequately considered, a question we've not asked deeply. "What time is it in your church?"

Sometimes a simple question opens new horizons. Questioning timing opens a dimension that has often been neglected. I am not referring to time management, but rather to a deeper sense of appropriate timing, a discerning of the opportune moment and conversely what does not "fit" in this season. We can learn how to dance church to the God-shaped rhythms of life.

Life is not static, linear, or uniform. It moves, oscillates, vibrates, and pulsates. A good church will find ways to harmonize with created and providential rhythms. Churches, like all organisms and organizations, develop through stages, experience seasons, and live in the cycles of creation (days and years). In this book, I attempt to open a new horizon on which we will see six rhythm strategies for wisely leading our churches so that we are more fruitful in ministry and ministry has more joy.

If you ignore rhythm, you can hurt your church by wasting resources on concerns that don't fit this time in your church's life. For instance, if you're a church planter in the early days it's not the time to develop policy manuals or refined processes. Much stress and guilt often come from attempting ministry that does not belong in this stage or season. In contrast, if we employ rhythm strategies, we can materially improve the quality of our ministry by releasing pressure and increasing focus. Churches that seize unique opportunities in a particular ministry rhythm find they increase their impact by focusing on what is timely. The effectiveness of "forty days" spiritual campaigns that were modeled after Saddleback Church's original demonstrate the power of focus. Adopting a rhythm approach can change the way you approach ministry because it lets you see it all through a new window.

Rather than feeling constant pressure to do everything all the time, you can flow ministry in life's rhythms if you pace yourself in natural cycles and oscillate between intensity and renewal. When churches release expectations that don't fit this time in their life, they reduce stress and experience more peace. When churches pursue unique opportunities that fit this stage of their organizational life or this season of their ministry, they find greater fulfillment in Christ. When church leaders seize timely moments, they find joy in accomplishing more of what God has for them in this place, at this time. They start having fun.

Rhythm is an intuitive concept that most people grasp from a few common observations, but it is common sense that can be most uncommonly applied. There are two main types of rhythm: *seasonal flows* and *regular cycles*. Flows are like stories with a beginning, a middle, and an end—a sense of linear development created by the arrangement of elements. Cycles are repeated sequences, such as a heartbeat, a sunrise, or the cadence of a drum—they are movements or variations characterized by regular recurrence or alteration. For instance, worship services are a weekly cycle for most local churches. They are regular, repeating, and consistent. In contrast, receiving a new pastor into a church begins a common season with its pattern of getting to know each other. Yet the time when a specific church will transition leadership can't be predicted like a sunrise.

Discovering the insights of rhythm may feel like a rediscovery, like déjà vu. When I explain the concept, people often say to me, "I've always known that but never put it into words." Or, "I knew that, but have never paid much attention to it." *Your Church in Rhythm* opens a window onto organizational timing, a dimension that we know is there but forget to take into account, to the detriment of our churches and our lives. Because rhythm is neglected, we do not ask crucial organizational timing questions that would improve our leadership. Too many churches are sterile, ineffective, in conflict, or bored. We are not celebrating life or having fun. Rhythm is a fresh way of thinking about church life; it's like opening the shade on a forgotten window. The forgotten window is time.

THE FALLACY OF THE GOOD, BALANCED CHURCH

Over the last forty-year generation, authors have created various paradigms for the mature God-honoring church. Years ago in *Sharpening the Focus of the Church* (1974), Gene Getz offered three vital experiences; then Rick Warren gave five purposes in *The Purpose-Driven Church* (1990);[1] then Willow Creek offered the six "Gs" defining commitments for church members in the 1990s.[2] Others have described eight characteristics (Hemphill) and nine marks (Dever) of a mature church.[3] Yes, churches should balance edification, evangelism, and exaltation; they should engage in vital worship, mission, and discipleship. Church-goers should magnify God, mature in Christ, minister to others, and engage in mission. Churches should be internally healthy and externally focused. Yet none of these models explicitly take into account the rhythmic life cycles of a church.

Other leaders, books, and conferences have recently helped churches become simpler in their organization (Rainer) and focused in their ministry (Stanley). We've been encouraged to consider the culture of our church (Corderio and Lewis) and how our church can prevail

(Pope). No matter what our culture or uniqueness, we are to be missional (McNeal), externally focused (Swanson), and building bridges of irresistible influence (Lewis).[4]

Without critiquing any one of these models in particular, or even comparing them, I'm making a metacritique that applies to all static models. None of these models are wrong, but how they are applied in the flow of ministry can create dysfunction. When we get to real-time, in-the-trenches ministry, how do we relate these models to what we are doing? If in any given time period we attempt to make our church fit each mark, letter, or purpose of a balanced church, we are in danger of toxic perfectionism. Rather, in any given period at our church, we need to focus on one element or another, but not on all of them.

Although it is often more implied than overtly stated, most authors who write about what makes a good, healthy church assume that a God-honoring church balances all the aspects of a mature church. In my earlier book, *Your Life in Rhythm*, I critique the notion of "balance" as it is applied to life in the sense of a "balanced life" or the attempt to balance work and life.[5] I argue that balance is unbiblical, impossible, and hurtful. The critique of balance in life has an analogue in the notion of a balanced church.

The concept of balance is flawed because balance happens in a frozen moment. Yet you cannot pause life to weigh its balance. Your ministry never stops; it is always moving and changing. There is no DVR remote control that will pause church.

Balance communicates a fixed value, as if there were some magical configuration of proportionate effort and time to a set of purposes or ministries that would determine a healthy church. But a well-run church should be unbalanced when examined in certain time segments: a week, a month, a year, or even a period of years. Although some things, such as the Gospel mission and the Lordship of Jesus Christ, are constant, ministry happens in time.

A rhythmic approach complements all these wise models of being and doing church by bringing the metaconcept of rhythm to bear on the discussion of how to form a God-honoring, Gospel-advancing local church. *Your Church in Rhythm* does not offer a paradigm to replace or compete with these other church models and approaches. Rather, it adds an often-missing view. Whether you are emergent, purpose-driven, organic, simple, programmed, contemporary, missional, creedal, seeker, traditional, reformed, or liturgical, you can be rhythmic too. Rooted in creation patterns and providential reality, rhythm applies equally well to churches, regardless of size or theology. Rhythm is an essential dimension of the created order; recognizing it gives crucial insight, whether your church is fundamental, evangelical, Catholic, denominational, liberal, or Pentecostal. If you grasp and deploy the six rhythm strategies outlined in this book, your church can experience less stress and better results, whether it includes twelve people or twelve hundred. As a complement to theological orthodoxy, organizational effectiveness, financial integrity, and missional clarity, rhythm brings better timing and this will improve our churches.

THE PERIL OF IGNORING RHYTHM

Pervasive Christian media create and feed unreasonable expectations in every area of ministry. As we read the blogs, go to the conferences, and download the podcasts, we hear about churches that are outstanding in various important aspects of ministry. We see what they are doing and become convinced that we too must be an outreach church; a praying church; a multiplying church that starts other churches; a recovery church; an emerging church to reach the next generation; a theologically deep church preaching the true Gospel; a technologically cutting-edge church using new media; a mission-minded church with a heart for the world; a sticky small-group church; a missional church with a heart for our community; a multisite church with many venues; and a stewardship church with a culture of generosity.

We think that something must be wrong with us—and something is wrong with us. In our attempts to "have it all" this year, we constantly push people to an artificial ideal. Ignoring rhythm can damage you and your church because you'll waste time on issues that are untimely. There is hope for better churches by sorting out good advice not only by its efficacy and value but also by its timeliness for this stage and these seasons of a church's life. As devoted church leaders, we are determined to take our churches to the next level while balancing everything in our personal lives. Yet, if we are honest, we struggle, sometimes deeply. We're doing our best to grow a "healthy, balanced" church, but our wheels are wobbling. We walk a balance beam, working our hardest to make sure each priority gets just the right amount of effort and time. But when do we ever get it just right? Ask yourself right now:

Has our church got everything in balance?

Are we reaching out enough?

Are we giving enough time to preparation of sermons and lessons?

How is our care and counseling ministry?

Are we leading well? Are we developing leaders effectively?

Are we praying enough?

How are our administrative systems and processes?

How are our ministries to children and youth?

Are our small groups vibrant?

How are we doing in following up with guests?

How is our communication with the church family?

How is our discipleship process?

Am I reading enough to grow personally?

Am I current on email and other correspondence?

Let me guess what you're feeling as you read this list: guilt, guilt, guilt. No one has ever told me, "Yes, our church is in perfect balance." We all know that even if we are feeling pretty good about our church at this particular moment, situations change so rapidly that a week from now we might be in chaos. It may sound radical, but consider this: trying to be a healthy, balanced church can actually be unhealthy.

Most of us want to build a great church, make a meaningful contribution, and enjoy ourselves along the way. But the stress of ministry drives us to anxiety, sleep disorders, depression, and even burnout. How many prescriptions are doled out each year to church leaders for antianxiety medications, sleep aids, and antidepressants? We want the insanity to stop.

THE JOY OF RHYTHM

No matter what kind of church you lead, thinking rhythmically will add value to your ministry because rhythm is a metaconcept that transcends size, style, and theology. When you focus on this time in your church and flow ministry in the God-made cycles of life, you can better advance Christ's mission with less stress.

Let's consider how ministry is like growing crops. To grow well crops need water, nutrients, good soil, and usually sunlight and protection from predators. But to support them properly we need to know what kind of crops we're talking about. Advice on how to grow a tomato is not the same as for how to grow a potato. We need to ask what kind of church we are growing. To give good advice on growing crops, we also need to know where they are being grown. What kind of soil is it? Clay or sandy, black or red? Are we near the equator or in a colder climate? Are we on a plain, in a desert, or down in a valley? We need to ask contextual, cultural questions about where we are growing our church. Are we in an urban area or rural? Is this a highly educated, affluent culture, or a working-class environment?

But along with those good questions, *Your Church in Rhythm* proposes an additional one: What time is it? What stage of the growing process are you in right now? Are you cultivating the ground for your crops? Are you planting them? Are they early in the growing season, just bursting out of the ground, or have they begun to bear fruit? Are they ready to be harvested or plowed under? What you need to grow crops well today depends on what time it is. Is this the first year to grow on this land or has this same crop been grown in this field for many years? If you try to plant tomatoes in the cold soil in January, they will die. Your garden will fail. Instead we want to be like the tree that "yields fruit in season" (Psalm 1:5). To continue the analogy, you may have heard a great seminar on tilling the soil where you learned an excellent technique for how to till well, but if it is not time to till the soil in your church, it will be unwise to try the excellent technique. You don't till the soil in the middle of the growing season.

So, with churches, we must take into account organizational life stages. Is this the time in the life of our church to plant another church; to rewrite the mission statement; to pay the pastor full-time; to launch a global mission; or to hire an executive pastor? Wise advice applied at the wrong time is foolish and can hurt your church. But well-timed advice causes your ministry to blossom.

The intent of this book is to offer you concepts and tools to make your church more effective and more enjoyable. After introducing you to the basic concept of rhythm, I will unfold the two kinds of rhythm: *kairos* and *chronos*. Chronos is measured time, such as on a watch or a calendar. Kairos is experienced time, such as the opportune time to invest or the right time to propose. You will discover that you can recognize two broad categories of kairos rhythms: stages and seasons. Whereas stages are longer periods in the life span of an organization, seasons are shorter periods lasting a few months to a few years. Churches live through both organizational life stages and ministry seasons. For example, a stage might be the early years of planting a church; a season could be a capital campaign. You will learn how to recognize what time it is in your church, and then identify your own stage and seasons.

When you understand and maximize kairos and chronos rhythms, it enables you to release expectations that don't fit this time while you seize unique opportunities in this stage of your church's life and anticipate what's next. When you recognize the five created chronos cycles, you can discover how to pace ministry better. This will allow you to establish life-giving habits and value-building traditions, as well as learn how to oscillate intensity and renewal in each cycle. Doing church in rhythm with the seasons and cycles of life will increase impact, reduce stress, and multiply joy for the leadership and the congregation.

Rhythm is the way life works and should inform the way our churches work. Christmas musicals, Lent/Easter, summer breaks, Mondays, and Sundays each carry their own distinct rhythms. Flowing with them gives us a more realistic and better church life.

Our heart is to see the Gospel of Jesus Christ advanced, to see churches multiply like rabbits so more glory goes to God. Rhythm can help us in this mission. By rejecting the insane pursuit of balancing all aspects of a church, you will free your church from impossible expectations. By choosing rhythm, you will invite your church to live in harmony with the flow of life—to be content in all circumstances, to make the most of the moments, to rejoice at all times—and to set your hope on what's to come.

The three kairos strategies apply to the two kinds of kairos rhythms: stages and seasons symbolized by the waves. The chronos strategies apply to the five chronos rhythms symbolized by the concentric circles.

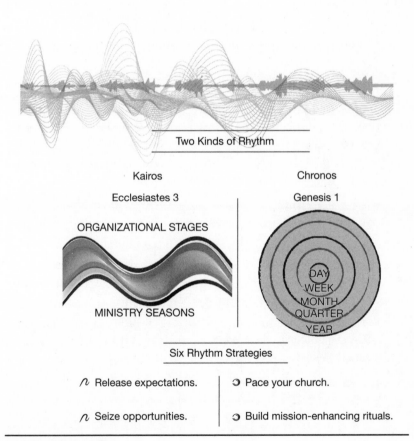

Two Kinds of Rhythm

Kairos

Chronos

Ecclesiastes 3

Genesis 1

ORGANIZATIONAL STAGES

MINISTRY SEASONS

DAY
WEEK
MONTH
QUARTER
YEAR

Six Rhythm Strategies

∿ Release expectations.   ↻ Pace your church.

∿ Seize opportunities.   ↻ Build mission-enhancing rituals.

Rhythm Overview

Each chapter of the book will end with a case study to which rhythm strategies can be helpfully applied. Each case will be presented in the format of the Rhythm Solution Process worksheet, which you can use to address issues in your own church. (A blank worksheet appears at the end of the Conclusion.) All six strategies can apply to each case, but I've often highlighted only a few because most churches can only focus on one or two steps at a time. As you get further into the book, the rhythm strategies will become clearer and you may want to come back to certain cases.

Rhythm opens the floodgates to innovation. I invite you to discover how to do church in rhythm.

Case Study #1
Dramatic Drop in Income and a Lawsuit

1. *Identify your issue or situation.*
Chris's church has a lawsuit against it from a receivership and is experiencing a dramatic drop in donations. Previously a large donor gave a tremendous amount of money to the church, but he was convicted of a Ponzi scheme and now the receivership is trying to recover over $1 million that he gave to the church. In addition, several other large donors have moved, left, or experienced financial reversal.

2. *What's the problem?*
The church is in a negative cycle that threatens its continued viability.

3. *What time is it in your church's life?*
Organizational stage: The church is thirty-eight years old. It was founded by a strong leader who left years ago in a church split. The church then suffered a series of moral failures. It is now in decline.

Ministry seasons: The current pastor has been serving over a decade with a small staff, but this new financial crisis has forced the church to let go nearly all the staff and cut back ministry to bare bones.

4. *Apply kairos rhythm strategies.*
Release expectations: The church leaders need to release expectations that the church will offer the array of ministries they have in the past. Even

a student ministry will be difficult to sustain. It's likely that the church will decline in size with the release of several staff and the cutback in ministry options.

Seize opportunities: The pastor can lead the people to seize the opportunity to return to the heart of Christ's mission. It does not cost money to evangelize or to disciple. Here is a great moment to return to the core mission of the church. Also this situation provides a great opportunity for the people of the church to do the ministry (Ephesians 4).

Anticipate what's next: The church can anticipate a few outcomes. One is that they will gradually rebuild with a healthy model, perhaps returning to a growth stage. Another option is that they could merge with a similar church.

5. *Apply chronos rhythm strategies.*
Pace your church (frequency and flow): The schedule of some ministry activities will need to be less frequent. What once might have been scheduled on a weekly pace now may be monthly or quarterly. Even producing a weekly worship guide may not be possible. The flow of ministry will become more organic and less organizational, more focused on daily life outside the walls with fewer programs of the organized church.

Build mission-enhancing rituals (traditions and habits): It would be valuable for the church to maintain rituals that they have known for some years as a way of sustaining continuity through a tumultuous time.

Oscillate intensity and renewal: The smaller team of people engaged in ministry will need to take times of renewal. With a smaller crew, it will be harder to get the work done in the same amount of time. Oscillation will be crucial for enduring ministry and health; otherwise the remaining leaders will crash when their energy runs out.

∾ EXERCISE

What situations, challenges, or problems in your church do you hope this book addresses? What would you like to gain from this book?

Your**Church**
in**Rhythm**

PART ONE

IdentifyingWhat Time It Is in Your**Church**

1

WhyDoChurch in**Rhythm**?

I f you are like me, you understand the feeling of wanting it all now. I want to be spiritually healthy. I'm sick to death of sinning. And I feel the same way about our church: I want it to be mature this week. I'm sick of our church's sin, dysfunction, and immaturity. My aim is for every ministry to be the best it can be. My heart is for us to be a praying, giving, worshipping, teaching, evangelizing, missional, community-impacting, global, loving, discipling church right now. It's not a bad dream, but I can drive my team, our people, and myself crazy with it. We beat ourselves up about what we are not doing or not doing well enough. On biblical measures of a good church and I want us to score well (actually at the top) on every scale, every year.

Some would ask what's wrong with this. It sounds noble. But it is an artificial idealism that ignores the reality of life cycles. It does not recognize our unique identity as a particular local church or this unique time in the life of our church. If we lead our churches to focus on every aspect of a mature church at every moment, it will hurt them. It will put undue pressure on people, piling on unnecessary guilt in the pursuit of an impossible goal. It will diminish our effectiveness because our efforts become diffuse, and it will rob us of joy because we are not celebrating what is going well.[1] There is a better way to do church.

I have claimed that a rhythm approach makes ministry more effective and enjoyable, but does the Bible have anything to say about rhythm? Do we see this idea working anywhere else outside the Bible? Is this a natural principle evident in the world? Will it enhance ministry? Is rhythm practical or is this just some interesting idea? We'll explore answers to these questions in this chapter.

A BIBLICAL SENSE OF TIME

We begin here by looking at kairos and chronos in biblical theology. God created chronos cycles when he made the world. They are rooted in the created order. In contrast, kairos rhythms flow from providence in the course of life. Genesis Chapter One and Ecclesiastes Chapter Three demonstrate these two types of rhythm. The account of creation establishes the five fundamental chronos cycles that order our temporal environment: annual, quarterly, lunar, weekly, and daily rhythms. King Solomon's famous poem artistically describes kairos seasons that we are to embrace as they come.[2]

In Ecclesiastes 3:1–8, Solomon portrays a rhythmic approach to life. In fourteen couplets, each a pair of opposites, he covers a wide range of human activity. Twenty-eight times, the word *time* is repeated as Solomon makes the point that God gives us rhythms by which we are to live, each appropriate to a unique season of our experience.

> There is a time for everything, and a season for every activity
>   under heaven:
> a time to be born and a time to die,
> a time to plant and a time to uproot,
> a time to kill and a time to heal,
> a time to tear down and a time to build,
> a time to weep and a time to laugh,
> a time to mourn and a time to dance,

a time to scatter stones and a time to gather them,
a time to embrace and a time to refrain,
a time to search and a time to give up,
a time to keep and a time to throw away,
a time to tear and a time to mend,
a time to be silent and a time to speak,
a time to love and a time to hate,
a time for war and a time for peace.

Although it is common to use Solomon's poem to validate balance, it does not support the theory that we should aim for a "balanced" life. Solomon is not saying to hold all activities in balance in each season, but rather to realize that different seasons call for different activities in a rhythm. For instance, he writes, "A time to tear down and a time to build." Obviously, one does not tear down and build at the same time. Instead he is saying there are times to tear down and different times to build.

The Hebrew word *time* as used here refers to more than chronological time; it refers to an occasion or season of time. Kairos describes experienced time, an opportune moment. Solomon challenges us that keeping and throwing away, loving and hating are not to be held in balance simultaneously but are to be fully expressed rhythmically at different times. When it is time to love your neighbor, love with all your heart; when it is time to hate injustice, hate it passionately. Live full out.

The poem opens with the most momentous events of human life: its beginning and its end—a time to be born and a time to die. We and every other living creature have a specific life span. Within the brackets of birth and burial come pairs of creative and destructive activities, private and public emotions. These are not times we choose, but ones we accept. The Anchor Bible commentary says: "Indeed, people do not decide when to heal, weep, laugh, mourn, lose, love, hate, or be in war or peace. These are occasions in which people find themselves, and they can only respond to them. All that mortals can do in the face of these times is to be open to them."[3]

We are not to be born and die, plant and uproot, weep and laugh all at once, but rather in rhythm at different times. Too often we skate over times of grief and skip past times of celebration when we would do better to fully enter those times, letting other priorities fade away for a season. When a fellow leader dies, it's time to grieve. When your son trusts in Christ or your daughter gets married, it's time to celebrate. Solomon's advice is to fully engage in each time. Throw parties. Have memorial services. Emotionally experience all that is there.

Each aspect of life has its time and season; thus, we need to understand the times (see 1 Chronicles 12:32). Living well involves having the wisdom to know the times and having the faith in God to accept that our times are in his hands (see Psalm 31:15). From God's eternal view, all times are "beautiful" or "appropriate" (see Ecclesiastes 3:11).[4] For instance, when the demographics of your community ethnically shift, your ministry needs to adapt. How can you do that well? There will be aspects of your current ministry to release and new kinds of ministry to embrace.

DEVASTATING CRITICISM: A SEASON OF REFLECTION

Recently, I suffered the most difficult criticism I've ever received because it came from an elder and his wife who had served on our staff and chose to resign over their concerns. This well-meaning, sincere couple came to believe that I was not fundamentally motivated by serving Christ, but at my core was self-interested. So they accused me of pride, lack of love, and self-promotion. That hurt. In their specific examples, situations were blown out of proportion and misinterpreted, but at my elder team's encouragement I took their concerns to God in serious self-analysis.

I did not see this season coming at all, but God used it for good. Rather than dismissing the conflict, our elders chose to work through a process that in hindsight was really wise. Although at the time it was agonizing, the Spirit of God revealed elements of truth in their concerns. I had to face pride in my heart, a lack of sensitive love when I am driving for the goal, and ways in which I choose language to make myself look good. God has grown me by helping me see myself more clearly, even though I suspect I will be working on these issues for the rest of my life.

Two of my elders spent hours in multiple meetings with this couple, talking through Scripture, praying together, wrestling with deeper issues about personal judgment of motives, reconciliation among brothers and sisters in God's family, and God's direction for our lives. Although in the end they remained entrenched in their view and left the church, these were not wasted hours. We parted in peace, with the couple appreciating how their issues had been heard and the care that had been extended to them.

When we shared the matter with the congregation during Sunday morning services, we were able to tell the story of how a difficult matter had been handled. The body had the chance to see accountability to an elder team and how conflict can be handled wisely, even if it ends with agreeing to disagree. My sermon that morning was a personal reflection on how God worked through the intense season of wrestling. In the weeks afterward, many in the body communicated their appreciation of our openness and transparency, of conflict handled well, and of inspiration to self-reflection on their own personal motives.

This brief season of leadership conflict was better embraced than dismissed. We could have quickly accepted the couple's resignations and as quietly as possible ushered them out the door, but in doing so we would have missed what God had for us in that unique time. Truthfully, I would much rather have expended that energy on what I saw as matters more beneficial to the mission, but God had other plans. His ways of growing us and our churches are often not what we would choose. But all times from God's larger view can be beautiful.

Solomon's point is that meaning in life can be found by seeking to fear God and to enjoy life. We are to accept what God has given and rejoice in his gifts. In such an approach we can replace despair and frustration with contentment (Zuck, 1994, p. 217). If we guide our

church in sync with God's rhythms, we can discover more peace, fulfillment, joy, and hope. God guides the world in providential seasons.
Although there is not a "correct" time to do everything, if we are living
in rhythm with God's timing, ministry will not be meaningless.
Everything will be "beautiful or appropriate" in its time, even difficult
experiences (p. 222). We will be like the firmly planted tree that yields
fruit in season and its leaf does not wither, but he prospers in whatever
he does (Psalm 1:3).

Models in the Bible, such as the nation of Israel with her periodic
feasts, Jesus with his sacrificial life, and the Apostle Paul with his zealous
devotion, illustrate lives of rhythm more than balance. For a season,
Jesus did carpentry and Paul made tents, but not in every season. Some
nights Jesus was in prayer the entire night, but not every night. At times
he sent the crowds away to be alone with his Father, but on other occasions when the disciples wanted to send them away, Jesus had the whole
crowd stay for fish sandwiches. Similarly, one simple model of how to
do ministry does not work. We need both to send the crowds away and
to invite them for dinner—not at the same time, but in rhythm at different times.

CHRONOS CYCLES FROM THE BEGINNING

Even the description of creation in Genesis 1 uses a rhythmic, Hebrew
narrative form. Each day follows a pattern, ending with the phrase "and
God saw that it was good." God created seasons, days, and years.
"And God said, 'Let there be lights in the expanse of the sky to separate
the day from the night, and let them serve as signs to mark seasons and
days and years'" (Genesis 1:14).

After the Flood, God promised that these patterns will continue.
"As long as the Earth endures, seedtime and harvest, cold and heat,
summer and winter, day and night will never cease" (Genesis 8:22). The
psalmist declares, "The moon marks off the seasons, and the sun knows
when to go down" (Psalm 104:19); and the prophet Jeremiah affirms,
"Even the stork in the sky knows her appointed seasons, and the dove,

the swift and the thrush observe the time of their migration" (Jeremiah 8:7). We should be at least as smart as storks!

God reflects the chronos cycles in how he set up Israel's rhythms of sacred and civil celebration. Every year, Israel celebrated an annual rhythm of festivals and sacrifices, including the holy Day of Atonement (see Exodus 30:10) and three annual feasts—the Feast of Unleavened Bread, the Feast of Weeks, and the Feast of Tabernacles (see 2 Chronicles 8:13). As God instructed, each year Israel was to make offerings tied to the movement of the moon. "This is the monthly burnt offering to be made at each new moon during the year" (Numbers 28:14). Annual and lunar cycles were complemented by the weekly Sabbath rest, based on the pattern of God's creation (Exodus 20:11).

In harmony with the annual, lunar, and sabbath rhythms, Israel also carried out daily offerings and times of prayer (Numbers 29:6). The Hebrews modeled a rhythmic life according to divinely inspired patterns. These spiritual rhythms corresponded to the natural rhythms formed in the created order. Only recently has science begun to discover the deep resonance of this rhythmic order.

RESEARCH INTO A NATURAL SENSE OF TIME

A casual survey of global cultures today and civilizations through history verifies that these cycles are not limited to one continent, language group, or historical time period. The rhythmic patterns revealed in God's Word are substantiated by scientific research that finds greater implications than we had realized previously.[5]

Chronobiology is revealing a new frontier of natural rhythms. It is the study *(logos)* of life's *(bios)* structure in time *(chronos).* Today, scientists such as Franz Halberg, the founder of modern chronobiology, are arguing that chronobiology represents a massive paradigm shift in how we approach life sciences.[6] A relatively new advance in science, chronobiology is the study of how living things keep time. Halberg sees science moving from a homeostatic paradigm (stasis) to a chronobiologic paradigm (rhythms).

In *Rhythms of Life: The Biological Clocks That Control the Daily Lives of Every Living Thing*, Russell Foster and Leon Kreitzman bring the insights of chronobiology to the general public. The authors describe how biological clocks allow organisms to adapt and respond to the rhythms that result from the movement of the earth. "Biological clocks impose a structure that enables organisms to change their behavioral priorities in relation to the time of day, month, or year" (2005). According to Foster and Kreitzman, "Today there are probably well over a thousand scientists working on the basic science of biological time. At least ten times as many are working on applying this information in medicine, agriculture, horticulture, manned space flights, and warfare." A new subdiscipline, chronotherapy, has discovered that a medicine's effect on you is determined by when you take it. In the foreword to *Rhythms of Life*, Lewis Wolpert writes, "Time is embedded in our genes" (Foster and Kreitzman, 2005, p. ix). According to Susan Perry and Jim Dawson in *Secrets Our Body Clocks Reveal* (1988), five major rhythms beat in our bodies, as shown in the following table.

Your Inner Rhythms

Type	Length	Examples
Ultradian	Less than twenty-four hours	Heartbeat; ninety-minute fluctuations in energy levels and attention span; brain waves
Circadian	About a day	Temperature; blood pressure; sleep/wake cycle; cell division
Circaseptan	About a week	Rejection of organ transplants; immune response to infections; blood and urine chemicals; blood pressure; heartbeat; common cold; coping hormones
Circatrigintan	About a month	Menstrual cycle
Circannual	About a year	Seasonal depression; sexual drive; susceptibility to some diseases

Although the circadian rhythm (from the Latin for "around a day") is the most well known, our rhythms vary slightly from individual to individual (23.6 hours, 24.3 hours, 25.4 hours, and so on). At times our internal clocks can get slightly out of sync with the environmental rhythm of a 24-hour day. But if all our individual cycles vary from a precise 24-hour day, wouldn't we in time get terribly out of sync? "Fortunately," write Perry and Dawson, "our bodies are able to reset themselves each day to the 24-hour rhythm, thanks to many powerful time cues. Chronobiologists call these cues *zeitgebers,* German for 'time givers'" (pp. 11–13). Scientists at the Hebrew University of Jerusalem have discovered a tiny molecule that may keep our rhythms in sync with the earth's rotation. These physical temporal markers create a bodily flow in harmony with the chronos cycles of nature.[7] "All of us in the developed world now live in a '24/7' society," write Foster and Kreitzman.

> This imposed structure is in conflict with our basic biology. The impact can be seen in our struggle to balance our daily lives with the stresses this places on our physical health and mental well-being. We are now aware of this fundamental tension between the way we want to live and the way we are built to live. It is hoped that our developing understanding of the basic biology will provide us with a means to resolve this fundamental dilemma of modern living. [p. 5]

Correlate Foster and Kreitzman's analysis with local church ministry. When we impose ministry patterns on our churches, we can be in conflict with our basic biology and with the temporal structure of our environment. When we ignore the deep structure of chronos cycles in our churches, we generate "noise" that puts people in tension with their created rhythms. An attempt to override basic life cycles leads to disaster. No wonder we feel so much stress in our churches. In a senseless syndrome, church people feel guilty because we cannot overcome natural cycles by sleeping less or by maintaining a constant pattern of ministry. But natural rhythms were never meant to be overcome; instead, we are meant to harmonize our church with them.

A rhythm approach is not a new artificial life management system to impose order on our churches. Instead, it recognizes the order built into our temporal environment. This is the way life works whether we want to fight it, ignore it, or embrace it. As scientists are discovering, living rhythmically leads to a healthier life. If everything around us functions according to natural rhythms, why don't we in our churches?

FOCUSED AND ENJOYABLE MINISTRY

Thinking rhythmically makes practical sense in church work as it does in all of life. Some of our insane "busyness" comes from trying to cultivate, plant, fertilize, weed, harvest, and repair the fences in every season. We are not meant to minister that way. Rhythm frees us to focus on one season at a time. Rhythm honors excellence and the sacrifice required for achievements while also providing times for renewal. A rhythm approach is more practical because it explicitly takes into account seasons and stages.

For example, at the start of a new church, you may build a large team to set up and take down chairs, sound gear, and children's equipment every week in an elementary school. Once you have a permanent space that team is no longer needed—or at least not such a big team. If you are between pastors, then it is time for a pastoral search, but once you have a pastor in place, there is no ongoing need for a search committee. Such overly obvious examples help us see that it makes sense to acknowledge that different stages and seasons of church life should lead us to focus on different issues.

For instance, is this the time in your church to reorganize your leadership structure? If you have just grown dramatically, then perhaps yes. But would you reorganize just because you attended a great seminar on a cool way to organize your leadership team? Or, in another example, is this the time for a citywide evangelism push? In one sense, it is always time for evangelism, but at this time in your church do you need to focus more on internal health or external growth? While you are giving energy to rebuilding your small groups should you also engage in a citywide major evangelism effort? Thinking rhythmically helps us ask these kinds of timing questions: Is this the right time to focus on this ministry, or do we need to concentrate on something else?

We are unnecessarily burning out our people and our pastors in the damaging pursuit of totally balanced churches. Members in a congregation get weary when they hear too many fervent messages urging that they come, serve, give, study, and attend one event, program, and meeting after another. Are they are all equally important right now?

Our constant and excessive expectations reduce our missional effectiveness, rob our people of joy, and rob us of joy as leaders. Unnecessary guilt is created by attempting the impossible ideal of providing proportionate effort to every dimension at all times. The same notion applies to major ministries, such as children, students, small groups, global missions, and worship. All should be strong and appropriately balanced, but to grow toward that ideal in the rhythms of a church's life, we must give extra focus at times to a certain ministry and not give that energy to others. Of course we already do this, but we beat ourselves up for it. A rhythmic model gives permission for "unbalanced" focus in seasons, and in fact advocates it.

If you free yourself from the false expectations inherent in trying to achieve the perfectly balanced church—and all the unnecessary burdens it places on you—that step alone will decrease your stress and relieve some of your frustration. At the very least, it will reduce your false guilt and increase your peace. Then you'll be ready to adopt rhythm as a better alternative.

WHAT TIME IS IT?

We have lots of activity and wonder why we have so little productivity for Christ. Being busy is obviously not the same as being fruitful. When you are trying to decide where to put your energy, you appropriately consider:

Your mission: Why are you doing what you are doing?

Your culture: How do things work in your region?

Your community: How are you making a difference for Christ?

Your uniqueness: What uniquely makes sense for your church?

Your organization: How could you simplify for effectiveness?

Your theology: Are you biblical?

Your communication: Are you being clear and consistent?

Your Church in Rhythm calls you to consider another dimension: What time is it in your church? In what stage are you in your life cycle as an organization? In what ministry seasons do you find yourself? How can you flow ministry better in the natural cycles of life? The two following tables summarize contrasts between the picture of a balanced healthy church and the better paradigm of rhythmic health portrayed in this book.

Balanced Health Versus Rhythmic Health

Balanced Health	Rhythmic Health
a pose	a dance
static	dynamic
rigid	flexible
you can have it all now	you can have much over time
control	embrace
setting goals	seizing opportunities
line	wave
all at once	over a lifetime
artificial/man-made	natural/organic/God-created
photograph	video

Advantages of Rhythm Versus Balance

Burdens of Balanced Health	Benefits of Rhythmic Health
Guilt over not giving adequate attention to every priority at every time	Peace in releasing expectations that do not fit this time and in setting a healthy pace for activities
Busyness in trying to push every purpose and ministry in every season and stage	Fulfillment in seizing the unique opportunities offered by each season and in building life-enhancing rituals
Stress in the attempt to keep everything proportionate at all times	Joy in embracing the blessings of each time and in the oscillation of work and rest
Despair of being stuck in the impossible pursuit of keeping everything in balance	Hope in anticipating a new season ahead and the ultimate rhythm sure to come

Rhythm enables us to build better churches by the power of God because we dance church in harmony with the cycles and seasons that come from God's hands. We can minister with less guilt and stress and be more effective. Rhythm offers a better way to do church.

✆ EXERCISE

What aspects of rhythm appeal to you? What benefits do you see inherent in the metaconcept of rhythm?

2

KairosandChronos **Rhythms**

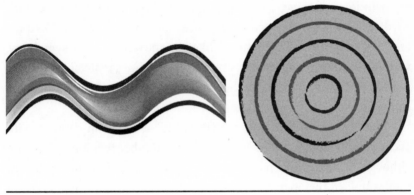

Kairos and Chronos Rhythms

The small town of Waco, Texas, was never a destination for me until my daughter, Melanie, decided to study vocal performance at Baylor University. None of her ability comes from her dad since I have no clue if a person is singing on pitch or not and can barely clap on the beat. But music reveals truths about rhythm. Music is beautiful because of both its meter and movement. It can carry both cyclical and linear rhythms. Some musicians argue that rhythm is at the heart of all music: patterns of sounds in sequence. Meter describes the cyclical beat of the music—its time signature or repeated sequence of sounds. Most songs have meter. Longer pieces of music, such as symphonies, also have movement. The music itself takes you on a journey. Movement, too, is a form of rhythm, but of a different kind. Like the rhythm of a story with a beginning, middle, and end, movement in a symphony is more linear than cyclical. It expresses progression more than repetition.

In this chapter, my goal is to help you grasp the two basic types of rhythm that I label kairos and chronos so that you will be able to powerfully employ the six rhythm strategies that are built on them. You can understand kairos and chronos by seeing them through a few windows: language, theology, and experience. As in music, life's rhythms come in two basic types: linear and cyclical. Kairos rhythms are linear, nonrecurring patterns like the movement of a symphony, whereas chronos rhythms are cyclical, recurring, predictable patterns like the meter of a tune. Churches live in both seasonal flows and cyclical patterns.

Most Christian theology describes time as linear in contrast with cyclical philosophies of time in paganism and other religions. However, although history moves in a linear direction, time itself flows cyclically. Better biblical theology recognizes the cyclical nature of time's flow in our created world. Time is both linear and cyclical; history is moving toward a *telos* (an end goal) but time flows in cycles, not as a uniform stream of moments.

THE WINDOW OF LANGUAGE

Depending on the period you are exploring, the actual usage of the terms kairos and chronos in Greek is not as distinct as I'm making it in this book. (For usage in the New Testament see Bauer, 2000.) As I'm using the terms, chronos is clock and calendar time, measurable and predictable. Kairos is experienced time, which is nonrecurring and not as predictable.

English words such as chronology, chronic, and chronicle arise from the Greek term *chronos*. Lexically, chronos relates to motion. It is a physical concept and thus quantifiable (Balz and Schneider, 1990–1993). Its origin is associated with the movement of celestial bodies. The term usually denotes time in general or a section of time, such as a part of a year. In the New Testament, chronos often refers to a span of time, but it can also be used to designate a special season (Kittel and Friedrich, 1964–1976).

In contrast, the earliest linguistic sense of the word kairos is the "decisive or crucial place or point." In the adage "Know the time" *(Kairon gnothi)*, kairos means "Know the critical situation in your life, know that it demands a decision, and what decision, train yourself to recognize as such the decisive point in your life, and to act accordingly" (Kittel and Friedrich, pp. 455–464). Kairos refers to the decisive moment when you can seize the opportunity in front of you. It carries with it a sense that destiny demands timely action.

In the Septuagint, the Greek version of the Old Testament, kairos shifts to a sense of divine appointment or a time of judgment. It can mean the "right moment"—a propitious hour. Though it is sometimes used in a purely temporal sense in the New Testament, kairos is also used for specific and decisive points in history and in an individual's life. When Jesus came he said, "The time (kairos) is fulfilled" (Mark 1:14).

For instance, in Ephesians 5:16, Paul says we are to wisely make the most of every "time" or "opportunity" (kairos).

Whereas chronos involves the quantity of time an activity takes, kairos looks at the quality of that time. Chronos is limited to regular measurements. Kairos considers events—such as the time a king reigned, the digital age, when communism collapsed in Russia, the time you fell in love at the beach, or when our church met in the school auditorium. These times are not fixed lengths such as hours, days, weeks, or even years; they are descriptions of an experiential period. When we pray for a time when peace will cover the earth, we are not talking about a date but a quality of life. A kairos moment can be as simple as the right time to say something sensitive to your small group or congregation. Proverbs 15:23 says, "A man finds joy in giving an apt reply—and how good is a timely word!" This kind of "right time" cannot be set on a clock; it must be discerned by the heart.

One way to understand the difference between kairos and chronos is to contrast the rhythms of the sea with the rhythms of the sky. The ocean has patterned but unpredictable, noncyclical rhythms to it. Sometimes the sea is calm; at other times waves crash onto the beach. Even with all our modern technology, we still cannot fully predict the sea's rhythm. We can be surprised by a tsunami that destroys a coastline or by a wave that knocks us off our feet while we're wading in the surf. The sky is different; it has a rhythm to it. The planets and stars move in cyclical, predictable patterns. We can look to the sun to know what time of day it is. The moon tells us what time of the month it is. The lengths of days and nights, tied to the tilt of the earth in relation to the sun, tell us what season it is. The stars tell us the time of year. We live rhythmically by both following the sky's patterns, which form our chronos rhythms (cycles), and by riding the sea waves of our kairos rhythms (seasons).

Christmas illustrates both kairos and chronos rhythms. Christmas falls on December 25 every year. That's an example of a chronos cycle. However, we move to kairos when we ask, "How did Christmas feel when you were six years old?" At six years old, Christmas was more than a date on the calendar. It was magical and delightful, a whole "time" (a season) of cookies, bright lights, shopping, decorating the Christmas tree, and anticipating colorfully wrapped presents.

THE WINDOW OF THEOLOGY

God created the chronos cycles. It was God who created our solar system with its specific astronomical configuration that generates our temporal cycles. No matter our country or century, every human lives in the same space-time world with the same chronos rhythms. God set the earth in motion revolving around the sun, thus forming the year. He spun the earth in a rotation that generates twenty-four-hour days and tilted the earth in regard to the sun to generate the seasons, or more concretely, the equinoxes and solstices. God also formed the cycle of the moon. From new moon to full moon, the lunar phases move in the same pattern approximately every 28.5 days as the moon rotates round the earth. So chronos rhythms refer primarily to four fundamental cycles formed by the way our sun, moon, and earth relate: day, month, quarter, and year. God also formed the week, but interestingly he did not arrange the sky to generate the week astronomically. There are biological patterns that follow a seven-day cycle, but they are not astronomically based.

In contrast with regular chronos cycles, God providentially guides the course of our personal lives and the history of the world so that we live in kairos rhythms. These are unique times such as the birth of a new church; the years when the church met in a school; rehabilitation after a moral failure; pastoral retirement; or moving to a new location. We ride the waves of life as they come. Whereas chronos cycles describe the temporal context of our environment on planet Earth, kairos rhythms describe patterns in the flow of our human lives in history. We do not usually get to pick kairos stages and seasons. They come in the providence of God. Our calling as leaders is to guide our churches well through what is required in each unique "time" for our church. When a leader decides to start a church, he looks for the "right time," which has little to do with a calendar. It has to do with insight and a sense of appropriateness.

THE WINDOW OF EXPERIENCE

In life we experience time in these same two fundamental kinds of rhythm. Some days feel like we are stuck in the movie *Ground*

Hog Day—forced to repeat the same day over and over. Every day the sun rises and sets. We eat, work, and sleep. Week after week we conduct worship services. It feels as if time is not moving forward but merely endlessly cycling, as if someone hit "repeat" and the same song is playing over and over again. And yet we also have times in our lives when it feels as if everything is changing; nothing is staying the same. We've moved, changed churches, and are establishing new friends in a new place. Life just keeps moving forward. Who knows what tomorrow may bring?

We experience some kairos rhythms as stages, from birth to childhood to adolescence to young adulthood to middle age, and so on. Life is also full of diverse seasons—from engagement to marriage, from pregnancy to birth, from growth to grief. Some of these we experience more than once, but never in the same way. No two pregnancies are identical. Kairos seasons are often unpredictable. Some can be anticipated, but many are total surprises. Although grief has a cycle, it is not based on astronomical movements. We do not know when it will come, and when it does each cycle of grief has unique features.

Church life is full of kairos ministry seasons. You may experience a capital campaign. That season has a pattern to it common to most churches and yet if you have experienced several capital campaigns, you know that despite similar patterned features, each is a unique experience. Likewise, the process of pastoral transition is a particular kairos season with recognizable features in an identifiable pattern.

In contrast, we experience chronos cycles as known and uniform. We can be sure that summer is coming. The sun will rise in the morning. Although we humans do not live through the same stage of life or experience the same season of joy or sorrow, we are all in the same year and month at the same time. In short, the five chronos cycles are shown in the following figure:

Orbital (annual):
Based on the earth orbiting the sun, about every 365 days.

Seasonal (quarterly):
Based on the tilt of the earth shifting, about every 90 days.

Lunar (monthly):
Based on the cycle of the moon, about every 29.5 days.

Sabbath (weekly):
Based on the creation pattern of seven days.

Rotational (daily):
Based on the rotation of the earth, about every 24 hours.

To lead churches rhythmically, we must consider all five created rhythms—annual, seasonal, monthly, weekly, daily—in harmony with one another. Part of the reason for our high stress levels is that we ignore the basic cycles of our planet. Fighting those rhythms creates frustration because the rhythms don't change; instead, we begin to burn out. We can find freedom from much of the guilt, stress, burnout, and excessive busyness in our churches by learning how to flow ministry in the natural cycles generated by the sun, moon, and earth.

These cycles are neither some artificial system created by the latest management author nor an artifact of one civilization or culture. These five cycles structure time in every culture of the world and have done so in every century of human history. Thus, no matter the size, flavor, or location of our church, we would be foolish to ignore these cycles or treat them as insignificant. They are obvious but we are blind to their significance. Our familiarity with the patterns of the year, quarter, month, week, and day can keep us from giving them the focused, conscious attention they deserve. We can maximize these chronos cycles for effective and enjoyable ministry by applying a few rhythm strategies.

With the three chronos strategies, we can first learn how to pace ourselves. Pacing involves frequency and flow. Second, we can not only pace ourselves in chronos cycles but also establish mission-enhancing rituals in each cycle. Third, we can learn how to oscillate intensity and renewal in each cycle. The three kairos strategies are equally powerful. Kairos seasons can be seized upon as opportunities to fulfill our mission and can be enjoyed for their blessing. In any given season, we want to release expectations that don't fit that time, as well as anticipate what comes next. The following table summarizes kairos seasons and chronos cycles.

Kairos Seasons	Chronos Cycles
Experienced time	Measured time
Quality of time	Quantity of time
Heart time	Clock/calendar time
Linear	Cyclical
Occurrence	Recurrence
Unpredictable pattern	Predictable pattern
Unique	Uniform
Progressing	Oscillating
Lifetime	Heartbeat
A symphony's movement	A song's meter

Kairos Seasons	Chronos Cycles
Hope	Ritual
Opportunity	Pace
Anticipation	Tradition
Phenomenological	Chronological

When you understand kairos and chronos, rhythm strategies will be more powerful in the life of your church. But to apply the kairos rhythm strategies, you must first discern what time it is in your church. In what organizational stage and ministry seasons are you living? This is what we will discuss in the next chapter.

Our second case presents a difficult kairos season for which all three kairos strategies offer solid wisdom to help the leaders navigate the church.

Case Study #2
Major Culture Shift with New Pastor

1. *Identify your issue or situation.*
George has recently assumed leadership of an existing relatively success-ful megachurch after its longtime pastor retired. George's predecessor had a laissez-faire style with little strategic planning, vision, or management oversight of the staff. He was a calm teacher with a degree in counseling. In great contrast, God made George a strong leader with a great sense of humor and a big presence. He quickly brought significant culture change that precipitated a crisis for many in the congregation.

2. *What's the problem?*
George's cultural shifts threaten his ability to remain the senior pastor and could fracture the church.

3. *What time is it in your church's life?*
Organizational stage: This church is thirty-one years old. It has reached the beginnings of a mature stage, having completed a major move into a

renovated commercial building. The intent in hiring George was to return the church to a new growth stage; however, it could tip into decline.

Ministry seasons: The church and George have passed the honeymoon season and are now in the early years of a new pastor bringing major change, including ending long-standing ministries.

4. *Apply kairos rhythm strategies.*

Release expectations: This church needs to fully release expectations: that George will lead as the previous pastor did and that the church will stay the same. The church leaders wanted change when they hired George, but when change came, many resisted. They also need to release the expectation that they should retain all the previous church members. Many will and should leave during the transition.

Seize opportunities: The church has a unique opportunity to redefine who it is and what it is about. It can create a new model and new culture for new stage of ministry.

Anticipate what's next: The church will stabilize. If George can weather the storms, then the church will move past conflict into acceptance of the new culture and the majority who remain will embrace the new direction.

5. *Apply chronos rhythm strategies.*

Pace your church (frequency and flow).

Build mission-enhancing rituals (traditions and habits): In a new culture, rituals provide tremendous power to carry and embody new values. The team could benefit from thinking creatively about new rituals to communicate and manifest the new culture.

Oscillate intensity and renewal.

✎ EXERCISE

In your own words describe and contrast kairos and chronos rhythms. What's an example of each?

3

DiscerningYour Organizational**Stage**

ORGANIZATIONAL STAGES

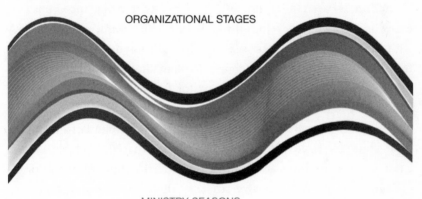

MINISTRY SEASONS

ow do you know when it's the right time? Investors ask this question every day. When is it the right time to get in and when do you pull out? When do you sell and when do you buy? It's all about timing. Homeowners ask similar timing questions about selling their home: Should we hold on and hope for a better market or sell now?

Timing requires discernment. Emotional stakes are even higher in personal relationships. When you have hot news to share with the person closest to you, whether it is really good or really bad, when do you break the news? Once a guy decides to marry a girl, he struggles with when to propose: *Do I do it tonight or wait for the "right" moment?*

Some people seem to have a sixth sense when it comes to timing. I have to work on the timing of a joke, but for my friend Don it is second nature. He does not even think about it. Socially, some people know when to tell a joke to break up a room at the right time in tension-releasing laughter; others paralyze a room in embarrassment with the same joke told at the wrong time.

Timing becomes powerful in a church when you can discern your organizational stage and ministry season, and then apply rhythm strategies. In the life span of a church, we go through several different stages with unique challenges and opportunities. Looking through the eyes of rhythm, we see church not as a static reality to be balanced but as a living organism that develops through time with natural ebbs and flows, with new rhythms for new seasons that call for different focuses. Is this the time in the life of our church to plant another church, to rewrite the mission statement, to pay the pastor full-time, to launch a global mission, or to hire an executive pastor?

As with other living organisms and other human organizations, local churches have a life cycle with somewhat predictable stages. Church kairos rhythms are most easily understood in relation to organizational stages and ministry seasons. These seasons and stages are more linear than cyclical. We move through them rather than repeating them.

Organizational stages are longer periods, similar to life stages such as adolescence, midlife, and retirement; they typically last from three to twenty-five years. These organizational stages are inception and early years, growth, maturity, decline, and then finally, death of the church. Ministry seasons generally last from one to thirty-six months. These include such seasons as conducting capital campaigns, building a new facility, launching or closing a major ministry or worship service, hiring or letting go a staff pastor, dealing with a leadership moral crisis, managing a burst of new growth, and planting a daughter church.

In this chapter, we will explore church organizational stages and discuss how to discern which one you are in. In the next chapter, we will consider how to identify your church's ministry seasons.

THE REALITY AND UBIQUITY OF LIFE CYCLES

Biblical theology tells us that the consequence of Adam and Eve's sin is death. Humans were made conditionally immortal. We did not have to die; sin brought death into our world. Until that final day when death is done, on this fallen earth we experience death. The Fall affected much more than just humanity. Death and decay riddled the planet. Plants and animals die. Scientists know the life cycle of most organisms; some are as short as twenty to thirty days (a housefly) and some are as long as centuries (a Sequoia tree).

Living organisms don't live uniformly through their life spans; rather, they develop and decline. They begin life as a seed or an embryo. Usually they start small, and grow larger and more complex. Seedlings become saplings and then trees; buds open into flowers. Past their prime, they begin to decline and die. They drop their leaves, stop producing fruit, get stiff, and rot. Many organisms have clearly defined stages in their life cycle, such as the caterpillar to the butterfly.

People also have life stages. Human beings have a life span of about 60 to 80 years. No human lives 150 years. We know the progress of human development from the zygote to embryo to the infant to the child to the adolescent to the adult. And toward the later years, we know biological systems slow down: our eyesight becomes less sharp, our hearing declines, and so much more happens that we don't want to think about. The point is that there is a life cycle.

In her books, *Passages* (1974) and *New Passages* (1996), Gail Sheehy shows how adults continue to live through stages, even after they are physically fully mature. In young adulthood, we try out independent life from our parents; then, for many, come marriage and children. After raising children, we hit a midlife crisis of identity and meaning. If we live long enough, we experience our senior years and some form of retirement. Each stage and each transition to a new stage carries with it dangers and opportunities.[1] Fuller Theological Seminary professor Robert Clinton's classic book *The Making of a Leader* (1988) popularized the concept of life stages in leadership theory. His studies of biblical and modern leaders have now been extended through the work of doctoral students to an ever-widening range of people. The studies confirm that leaders develop through identifiable stages. Clinton encourages building a time line to envision how God has worked, and will likely work, to shape a person over time.

Organizations also have life stages. They usually begin as an idea in an entrepreneur's head. Capital is raised. A small location is secured. Simple promotions are made. Doors are opened and the first dollar is made. As organizations mature, they develop more structure, sophistication, and systems. Without some intervention, organizations will peak and then decline. According to Peter Drucker, "Historically, very few businesses were successful for as long as thirty years in a row" (2008, p. xxxi). He does not mean that they ceased to exist, but that they entered a long period of stagnation from which it was rare to recover. Many factors come into play, but the death of an organization is not always a bad thing in an overall economic view.

Since Mason Haire's 1959 work *Modern Organization Theory*, scholars have applied a biological model of organizational growth and development to companies and other organizations, including schools and hospitals. Early theoretical literature has now been buttressed by empirical studies. Although there is no consensus on the exact number of stages (studies vary from three to ten, with substages as well), a few principles are consistent. First, stages are sequential in progressive development. Second, an organizational stage involves a broad range of the organization's activities and structures, not just an aspect of the operation. Third, the sequential progression is not easily reversed. In general, life cycle models assume that organizations move from inception to growth, to maturity, to decline and death or redevelopment. However, unlike living organisms such as plants and animals, organizations can avoid death by restarting with new leaders and a fresh direction.

As with living organisms, it is possible to predict common issues at each stage of an organization's life. A premise is that priorities, opportunities, and dangers vary depending on the stage of the business. In *The Five Life Stages of Nonprofit Organizations,* Judith Simon (2001) argues that the "life stage model is a powerful tool for understanding—objectively—your organization's current status and preparing to move it ahead to the future."

By understanding organizational stages, nonprofits can put problems in context, effectively manage transitions from one stage to the next, keep the organization on track, and monitor warning signs of decline. Thus, you can avoid unnecessary struggles and be prepared for typical issues. Each stage offers wonderful opportunities and treacherous threats. The following list shows traits that are common to each typical organizational stage.

Inception and Early Years
   One-man show; founder bearing bulk of responsibilities
   Single product
   Prime concern: securing financial resources to survive
   Informal communication and minimal structure or systems
   Centralized and personal leadership
   Focus on the vision, the big idea, the dream
   Secure initial locations and staff
   Strong commitment and purpose with uncertain future

Growth
   Rapid expansion
   Need for planning with increased size and complexity
   Felt need to create policies and procedures for stability
   Delegation by founder of responsibilities and staff management
   More formalized structure emerges
   Beginning of functional specialization and departmentalization
   Need for more space

Tension between founders and new board members

Danger of overextension with personnel, finances, and product lines

Maturity

High confidence in who the organization is and what it's about

Strong results orientation

Peak of influence and scale

Rules and procedures are formalized and often rigid

Well-defined and less flexible structure

Reduction of innovation, slower to change

Multiple product lines

Inertia of sustaining activities and programs and products

Need for good change-management practices

Decline

Self-deception, unrealistic optimism

Inflexibility, rigidity

Short-sightedness

Poor communication

Overconservatism, conformity, group-think

Commitment to past strategy

Rivalry among factions, scapegoating, blaming, polarization

Nostalgia for past achievements

Need for revitalization

Death or redevelopment carries its own challenges. Will you convey the assets to another group? Will you dissolve the organization entirely? Will you reinvent the organization as something new? A church can be renewed, brought back to life. British business author Charles Handy popularized the sigmoid curve (originally a mathematical concept) in his book *The Age of Paradox* (1995). Handy showed that paradoxically an organization is in the greatest danger when it is most successful, at the top of the curve. Here is an illustration of

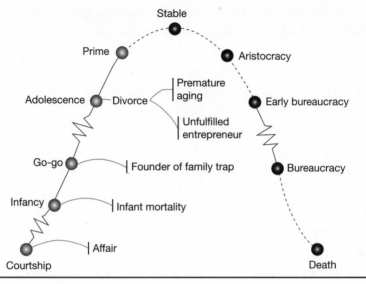

Organizational Life Cycles
Adizes, Ichak. *The Pursuit of Prime* (Santa Barbara, Calif.: Adizes
Institute Publications, 2005), p. 8.

organizational life cycles from Ichak Adizes, thought leader of the
Adizes Institute, one of the world's leading experts on organizational
performance and change.[2] According to Handy, leaders want to make
changes to start a new curve at the stable point before aristocracy
sets in.

There can be great variation in focus during different life stages.
Consider the unique priorities and issues at different stages in the life
of Israel. In Abraham's day, the nation was founded. A big obstacle was
infertility and the priority was a son to carry on the family. Water wells
were a big deal. Abraham fussed with Lot and fought kings of the plains.
Under Isaac and Jacob, the focus was on building a family. What a difference four hundred years later when they had multiplied but were
slaves in Egypt. The issue was deliverance, and God used Moses to
accomplish that. He demonstrated great faith, incredible leadership
under duress, and the ability to delegate as his father-in-law Jethro

advised (Exodus 18). After Moses, Joshua led Israel with a major priority of taking the land by military force and dividing it among the tribes. Under the prophets, epitomized by Samuel, the issues were faithfulness to the covenant while avoiding false gods. The people demanded a king and God gave them Saul, whose focus was fighting battles with the Philistines. David finalized the conquest in a major growth phase during which being a good solider was crucial to success. Solomon solidified the nation by successfully building the temple in the nation's mature phase. When he died, the decline began with his son Rheoboam. The nation divided into Judah and Israel, and was never reunited. Eventually, both were taken into captivity in Babylon and the nation ceased to exist as an independent state. After seventy years, they returned and men such as Ezra and Nehemiah led them in a rebuilding phase. Restoring the laws of the nation and rebuilding the walls of the city were the focus. God remained the same holy God, but at each stage the priorities, dangers, and opportunities were very different. It is this way with local churches too.

ORGANIZATIONAL STAGES IN CHURCHES

Like living organisms, human beings, and other organizations, churches also have life spans. No individual local church lasts forever. Some are short-lived, but many last for over a hundred years; few continue beyond several hundred years. It isn't as important to categorize our seasons and stages as it is to understand what time it is and to live in sync with our current organizational stage.

An additional complexity is presented by the fact that larger organizations are collections of suborganizations, each of which has its own life cycle. It is likely the suborganizations are at different stages of their life cycle. Think of children's ministry, student ministry, small groups, or worship. One team may just be launching while another is maturing.

What are typical organizational stages in the life span of a local church? Because the church is both an organism and an organization, we are not surprised to discover the same fivefold generic pattern: birth, growth, maturity, decline, and death. Most of the features of each organizational stage listed here also apply to local churches, but a church's expression of the stages is unique. Martin Saarinen, former Director of Continuing Education at Lutheran Theological Southern Seminary in Columbia, South Carolina, developed an eight-stage model for a congregation's life cycle in his solid work for the Alban Institute. In *The Life Cycle of a Congregation* (1986), he sees four stages in an overall growth phase—birth, infancy, adolescence, and prime—and four in an overall declining phase—maturity, aristocracy, bureaucracy, and death.[3]

The five generic stages have been refined by veteran church consultant George Bullard.[4] Based originally on research for his dissertation, Bullard has labeled ten organizational stages for a church correlated with four fundamental congregational issues: visionary leadership, relationship experiences, programmatic emphases, and management accountability. In Chapter Five of *Pursuing the Full Kingdom Potential of Your Congregation* (2005), he notes the significance of identifying your church's life stage. "Over the years, I have found the life cycle to be one of the best learning tools for congregational leaders. Properly understood, the life cycle provides an excellent assessment for a congregation and allows it to know its starting point, and the issues it must address, to be able to spiral forward to the next cycle in its spiritual strategic journey" (p. 76).

Bullard analyzes next steps for churches at each organizational stage and shares how to intervene in order to achieve full Kingdom potential at www.SSJTutorial.org. The following helpful chart displays his analysis of the stages correlated with the four major congregational issues that define the stages.

You have likely experienced one or more of the following stages.

Inception of a New Church

God puts a vision in a church planter's heart. He dreams of a new church in a new place where he will reach many people for Christ. In

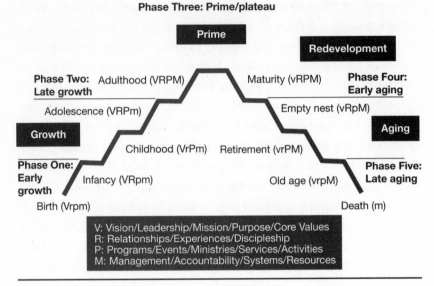

The Life Cycle and Stages of Congregational Development
Copyright 2001 Rev. George Bullard, D. Min.

preparation, he reads books on the topic, surfs the best websites, and goes to church-planting conferences. He puts his plan on paper. No church will exist without a team of people and financial resources, so he recruits leaders and raises money.

A launch strategy is designed and the countdown begins. The team settles on a name and logo with tag line. Marketing plans are executed while prayers are lifted up every day. The young team holds preview services, getting ready for Sunday One. People come to the grand opening, and soon the church is rolling.

The early days are filled with setting up church every Sunday in a school or another temporary facility. Every single person is engaged because they have to be or church services simply would not happen.[5] There is high ownership expressed in financial giving and in volunteer time contributed (Tidsworth, 1992).

The devil often attacks churches in their infancy with an internal moral crisis. In the Book of Acts, Chapter Five, we see this in the sad case of Ananias and Sapphira. As leaders in the early church they, along with others, sold property to finance the ministry. But they chose to lie, saying they had sold more property than they had. God took their lie very seriously and struck them dead. Their story echoes the sin of Achan in Joshua, Chapter Seven. The nation of Israel had just begun to take the Promised Land with amazing God-given success in the first great battle against Jericho. Although the people were to take nothing, Achan stole property from Jericho. This troubled the whole nation, causing their defeat in the second battle against the little town of Ai. Joshua dealt severely with Achan and his family. As a new church, you must deal with early sin in the leadership decisively. Take it seriously and act quickly for the sake of the whole body and the mission of Christ.

The Church Grows

If by God's grace the church grows in size, the organization will move to a growth stage. For local churches, this shift often happens in concert with purchasing land or building a first facility. The founding pastor must delegate significantly in the move from inception to growth. He cannot lead over coffee with his handful of good friends. He cannot continue to make the copies, set up the chairs, and play keyboard. New skill sets are required for totally new issues. Now a staff must be built, whether paid or not. Leaders must manage people. Often the number of people involved requires more sophisticated systems for tracking people, events, and money.

Coordinating all the emerging ministries and keeping everyone going in the same direction becomes challenging. Depending on the rate of growth, the staff must be restructured several times. Who do you put on which leadership teams? As a church increases in size, it outgrows the capacity of some of its original leaders. These are godly, wonderful people, but they may simply not have the horsepower to lead a larger organization. The woman who could care for ten children may not be the one to oversee one hundred. It is painful to move a good friend out of a ministry role, especially if he or she founded the church with you and sacrificed greatly to get it off the ground.

The Church in Maturity

At some point, you realize that systems are in place and have now been working for a while. Your annual calendar becomes more routine rather than a blank slate. You refine events and programs rather than creating them. Even as individual team members come and go, staff structure is stable. The church is known in the community. You are making a difference. You may finish building out your campus with facilities. You are at your prime with maximal influence.

At this stage, you look outward at partnering with other churches and organizations. You give more attention to global missions around the world as you have the size and stability to export people and funds. You lend leadership to larger outreaches in your community, starting ministries with other churches and community groups outside your church. Depending on the age of the primary pastor, you may begin to ask questions about succession. When is it time to step down from primary leadership and pass the baton? Who will come next?

Decline of the Church

No local church has lasted since the time of the New Testament. None of the seven churches in the Book of Revelation remains today. This is not necessarily a bad thing. Christ's church endures, but not individual local expressions. Local churches have a life span in a fallen world marked by death. Local churches should be sending out seeds to plant many other local churches. While the original local church will decline and die, its ministry impact lives on in daughter and granddaughter churches. The point is not to grow larger and larger for hundreds of years, but to reproduce many times over. It would be bizarre for a flower to grow larger and larger, but wonderful for it to reproduce into a field of flowers. Or for a tree to become a forest. The better dream for a local church is not to grow larger indefinitely or last for millennia, but to give birth to a movement of multiplying churches.

Eventually, every local church diminishes in size. In decline, your resources lessen. With less money and fewer people, ministries must end. It's easy to get discouraged. However, usually one young leader or two want to take the church in a new direction. You can embrace renewal or progressively decline. It is not always clear which is the better option. In decline tensions rise, conflicts deepen, and factions can form.

Death or Renewal of the Church

At some point in the decline, those leaders who remain question the future of the church. Can we even continue to afford to pay a pastor, the mortgage, the utilities? But the death process for a church can be lengthy, especially if the land and building are smaller and all paid off. "The difference between business and church is that no business is more than three years away from failure, as we've all painfully seen this last year. A church, on the other hand, takes two decades to die. You can hardly put a stake through its heart."[6]

When the remaining leaders finally face their true stage, various options emerge. They can sell the property and give the money to a worthy Kingdom cause. They can give the property to another church. They can invite a young leader to replant and restart the church, as if from scratch. Or they can continue to pay the bills for as long as possible, until those remaining eventually die.

THE IMPACT OF CRISIS

In local churches as well as in other organizations, sometimes life stages are not so straightforward and linear. We can overgeneralize our own lives by saying simply that people grow up, get married, raise kids, retire, and enjoy grandkids. However, that cycle can be interrupted by divorce, death, infertility, or singleness, whether by choice or not. Rarely does life follow a straight path, and yet our lives do move forward. Our churches do as well.

In ecclesiastical life, sometimes a church wracked by conflict splits into two congregations. A new church is formed and the original church hemorrhages. Often the new church is short-lived because it was started in bitterness, anger, and resentment. At times, the original church takes years to recover, and with great pain. It's like a divorce for the church family with many ruptured relationships.

When a church has had a dynamic strong leader as pastor for decades, especially the founding pastor, the transition to the next pastor can be a shift to an entirely new church. The new pastor will be younger, sometimes much younger, with fresh ideas and a different personality. Over decades, the church formed its culture due in large part to the influence of the previous strong leader, but now the new pastor brings a new culture. Many people who preferred the older pastor leave, and one hopes, many new people come, attracted by a fresh voice. If the new pastor survives and thrives, he will lead the church to such renewal that it is like a restart with fresh vision and ideas. This will not take the church back to an inception stage (unless it loses nearly everyone), but can put the church back into a growth stage where there is once again invention of new ministries, systems, and structures.

A similar phenomenon in a mature or declining church occurs in the wake of huge crises or a major transition. For instance, if a church leaves a denomination or significant affiliation, the change can be so profound as to move the church into a growth mode once it passes through the transition. A moral crisis in the life of the key leader can lead to pastoral transition. A major theological shift, such as to become evangelical, Pentecostal, Calvinist, or liturgical (when it was not previously) can signal a new beginning for a church.

Sometimes a major change is forced not by factors in the congregation or the pastor, but in the community itself. When a downtown neighborhood experiences ethnic changes, the complexion of the church also changes. Some churches relocate to the suburbs. Others re-create themselves as ethnic or multicultural churches.

On a larger canvas, we cannot control our external context. Any one of us could experience a massive natural disaster, horrific economic downturn, or even terrorism. Should war come to our homes, life and ministry would dramatically change. Only God knows the spiritual, economic, and social context in which he will place us to serve him. Each context offers opportunity for the Gospel. America is currently in an economic downturn, but the effect in Detroit is much more intense than in Dallas. Wise leaders will ask: *What time is it in our church and what time is it in our community?*

DISCERNING YOUR CHURCH'S STAGE

It is difficult to discern your church's time when no watch tells it and no calendar marks it. You can build from the reality of organizational stages in order to recognize common church stages. But how do you discover your own rhythms? Where is the timepiece that shows your kairos time?

My best advice is to pray. Invite the Spirit of God to illumine you, to open your eyes to this time in your church. Include others in your discernment. When dealing with a communal reality such as a church, you will see deeper and farther with others. Discuss and wrestle with it. Make a stab at identifying a possible stage; debate it with other leaders. Compare your church with the descriptions of common life-cycle stages. Examine yourself to see if you are squarely in the midst of a life stage or perhaps transitioning from one to another.

In my church, we are engaging in a time of discernment, including getting outside help from a consultant to more clearly grasp our unique identity so we can sharpen missional clarity. We believe this is just the help we need at this stage of our church's life. I'll share more of our story later. But in this process of self-discovery, I hope that we will also more deeply discern our rhythms.

Our third case offers what appears to be a bad kairos stage that must be named and then good leaders can prayerfully see and seize latent opportunities.

Case Study #3
A Stagnant Church Is Leaderless Between Pastors

1. *Identify your issue or situation.*

2. *What's the problem?*
Frank's church is stuck. He's been an elder in the church for twenty years. They have hovered at around 175 in attendance the entire time he has been there, but more recently attendance has dropped to about 125. In those twenty years, he has seen three pastors come and go. Now they are without a pastor. Their heart is to reach their community with the Gospel of Jesus Christ.

3. *What time is it in your church's life?*
Organizational stage: The church is in a mature stage in danger of having just entered a stage of decline.
Ministry seasons: They are in an interim season between pastors.

4. *Apply kairos rhythm strategies.*
Release expectations.
Seize opportunities: The church has some serious questions to face about what opportunity they want to seize. The writing may be on the wall in terms of their future viability apart from drastic change. Now is the time to seize the opportunity to re-envision the future of the church or envision how to bring it to a close well by inviting another church to absorb them or gifting the property to a church plant. If they want to move into a new growth phase, that will significantly impact the kind of pastor they hire.
Anticipate what's next: Either a new growth phase that will be uncomfortable for many but exciting for some, or the church will end well.

5. *Apply chronos rhythm strategies.*
Pace your church (frequency and flow).
Build mission-enhancing rituals (traditions and habits).
Oscillate intensity and renewal.

✑ EXERCISE

Consider the following questions as guides to help you discern what time it is in your church or in your specific ministry, and just as important, what time is it not.

Age: How long have you existed as a church?

Tenure of the current senior pastor or senior leadership group, board, committee?

Length of time in your current location and in your current worship space?

Evaluate yourself against typical signs of typical stages; see Figure 3.2 and Bullard's website.

Have the demographics of your community around the church shifted significantly? When?

What is the average age of members in your church? Is it increasing, decreasing, or stable?

Have you experienced major churchwide conflicts in the last few years?

Have you changed denominations, affiliations, or theological camps?

Growth of the church: Is the size of the church stable and for how long has it been stable? Is it declining? Or increasing? At what rate? For how long?

Plot your church on the typical organizational curve provided on the following page. Then test your ideas with others. Ask other church leaders what they think. Invite them to respond to your hypothesis.

1. Our church's likely organizational stage is: _____

   _____

2. The following markers indicate our stage: _____

   _____

   _____

Some church leaders find it helpful to sketch a time line of their church to determine its organizational life stage. When did your church begin?

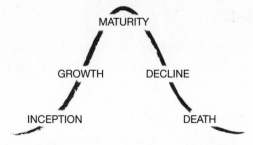

Include only major factors, such as changes of the lead pastor, moves to new facilities, significant crises or surges forward, and new campuses or services. Indicate worship attendance trends. Sometimes a quick look at the church's history on a one-page time line is revealing.

4

RecognizingYour Ministry**Seasons**

ORGANIZATIONAL STAGES

MINISTRY SEASONS

D uring difficult times my mom has consoled me with her proverbial sayings. When I shared my stress over writing a book, she gave me her classic momily, "Bruce, remember, you are just in a season." The more I thought about it, the more I realized that I'm always in a season. How could any of us, or any of our churches, ever *not* be in a season? Of course, my mom's advice still makes sense, because this current season, however difficult it may be, will always yield to another season that will be different, whether it is easier or not. Although "this too shall pass" may be a cliché, it remains a fitting adage. My intent in this chapter is to help you discern ministry seasons by understanding their characteristics, recognizing features of common ministry seasons, and using commonsense markers to identify seasons.

THE NATURE OF MINISTRY SEASONS

How are ministry seasons distinguished from organizational stages? Seasons present a shorter kind of kairos time. Generally, organizational stages run from three to twenty years, while seasons are shorter, from about three months to three years. Some times are in the middle and can be considered either stages or seasons. How you label them is not nearly as important as identifying that you are in a particular kairos time.

Stages affect every aspect of a church, while seasons might affect only some aspects and some groups. For instance, some seasons are departmental: in a larger church if the middle school pastor or director leaves it will create a transitional season for those engaged in middle school ministry but probably not for the rest of the church. Some individuals may not even be aware of it.

You are usually in only one organizational stage at a time or transitioning between stages, but it is common to be in more than one ministry season. You could be in the season of launching a new service or venue when a board member falls into sexual sin and you begin a second season of dealing with moral failure. Now you have at least two seasons going on at the same time. There are many ministry seasons, such as growth, conflict, building a facility, and hiring a pastor.

Another difference between stages and seasons is repeatability. Generally, stages are more linear than seasons. Most church leaders will only live through an organizational stage once because of the length of time they take and because one stage tends to follow the next. An exception is leaders who stay long enough into a maturity stage to experience a restart into a new growth stage with fresh leaders and a new direction. However, it's also normal for leaders to experience a certain kind of season several times. Some we would rather not reexperience, such as dealing with financial crisis, but others are more enjoyable, such as launching major new programs, services, or approaches. Whether they seem positive or negative, all seasons can be redeemed for Christ's mission.

Organizational Stages	Ministry Seasons
Longer; last three to twenty years.	Shorter; last three months to three years.
Every aspect and area is affected.	May impact only one ministry area.
Church is in only one at a time.	Church can be in several simultaneously.
Typically linear, usually happen once.	May be experienced several times.

To better understand the nature of ministry seasons, it's helpful to distinguish them from chronos cycles, which could seem similar. The key to the distinction lies in the fundamental difference between kairos and chronos rhythms. Remember, chronos rhythms are cycles built into the temporal structure of creation based on the movements of the earth, sun, and moon. Summer is a cycle that recurs every year with absolute predictability. In contrast, kairos seasons happen in the providential flow of history; some seasons can be anticipated and planned, others are surprises. Launching a new worship service would be a planned season with great intentionality. In contrast, Christmas (although it is described in ordinary English usage as a "season," as in "the holiday season") is a chronos cycle that recurs annually, not a kairos season.

All chronos cycles are completely predictable and universal. Some kairos seasons are planned and thus predictable, but others come as complete surprises. Rarely do we see moral failures coming. And although we plan capital campaign seasons, we must move quickly to deal with a crisis that initiates an unanticipated season. Once we had a child escape from our Mother's Day Out program. Even though the child was only out for five minutes and the parents were on the property, the mom involved was a self-described psycho-protective mom. She called the state to report us to the relevant authorities. Our operations pastor, who manages risk for us, immediately called our attorney, who guided us. Thankfully this did not turn into a drawn-out legal matter, but it could have.

Although a kairos ministry season may be unexpected, once it starts its cycle usually follows a common pattern. After you've lived through one a few times, you come to realize that. For instance, in the situation just described there is a pattern: an incident occurs; leaders become aware of it; reactions run from minimizing it, to blowing it up out of proportion, to reality; facts are gathered; expert advice is solicited; proper authorities are informed; a meeting is held with those involved; corrective measures are established; those measures and the situation are communicated to those who contributed to it and could prevent another similar incident in the future. Then a leader circles back to those who raised the complaint (in this case the parents) to ensure that nothing remains unresolved.

Ministry seasons are not based so much on chronological age as they are identified by significant experiences. A season is a period of time characterized by unique features that set it apart from other times in our lives. What makes it a season is its magnitude in terms of how many people are affected for how long and how deeply. If a sermon series becomes a campaign, it may be a ministry season. When a focus becomes a directional change, it may be a ministry season. When you identify a period of time as a season, you can apply rhythm strategies that will enable you to maximize that season for the Kingdom. If you are unaware that you're living through a season, you may miss opportunities and waste resources. Given the reality of ministry seasons as shorter times with predictable flows, what can help us discern them? The following section describes various kinds of ministry seasons. When you can recognize common seasons, you will be better able to discern ones that are not as common.

RECOGNIZING COMMON MINISTRY SEASONS

It is difficult to classify ministry seasons because they are so diverse and numerous. Are you starting a new outreach? Moving into a new facility?

Opening a new service? Are you rehabilitating after a conflict or recovering from a moral failure in leadership or experiencing huge growth? Have you buried a much-loved pastor? There are thousands of ministry seasons. Some seasons are restful, others are taxing.

Grief is, unfortunately, a common experience. A typical pattern of grief was first articulated by Swiss-born psychiatrist Elisabeth Kübler-Ross, whose book *On Death and Dying* (1969) became a foundational text in the study of grief. Most psychologists and counselors today accept her model of five basic stages of grief: denial, anger, bargaining, depression, and acceptance. These stages can occur in different orders and with varying degrees of intensity. But when we are in a season of grief, we cannot live well if we attempt to ignore the grief cycle.

Churches experience seasons of grief after a congregational loss. When a respected pastor or leader leaves, a church walks through a season of grief. If that leaving was forced or sudden, the grief can be more intense. When a student ministries pastor had to leave our church rather quickly because he had mishandled matters, the students who loved him grieved. If the remaining leaders had tried to just pick up and go on as if nothing had happened, they would have injured the students by not recognizing the "time" in the group. Since that youth pastor chose not to come see the students again, some students felt unsettled by a lack of closure. Good leaders guided the students in writing cards to the pastor. They provided the cards and offered to deliver them. Students were encouraged to write emails and send Facebook messages, telling that pastor how much he had meant to them. The group needed to take time to grieve. This was a short grief cycle for all except those who were closest to the former pastor, but it illustrates the need to discern the time, to recognize a ministry season and what it requires.

Not every ministry season is as well understood as the grief cycle, but several have been studied. There is good information out there for church leaders on how to best walk through common challenging ministry seasons. For instance, you can find wise counsel on the pattern of exiting a pastor well and the process of hiring a new pastor, including guidelines for a pastoral search committee. When a new pastor comes to an existing church, it is advisable for both the congregation and the church to learn about the season of a new pastor's first year. What can the church expect and what can the pastor and family expect? Consultants have developed businesses around ministry seasons. Perhaps the most familiar are stewardship consultants who have mastered the pattern of capital campaigns. Other consultants offer help with interim seasons between pastors; building facilities; branding a fresh identity (communication consultants); and launching new churches (church planters); or starting multisites.

Another category of ministry season is "starts." Whether you are starting a new service time, ministry, or outreach, you must engage in a change process. Most people resist change, so they need help through it. Change requires communication and is best handled by following a change-management process. Jon Kotter (1996) famously developed an eight-step change management process, which many leaders have been glad they followed and many more have wished they had. These are the eight steps:

1. Establish a sense of urgency.
2. Create the guiding coalition.
3. Develop a vision and strategy.
4. Communicate the change vision.
5. Empower a broad base of people to take action.
6. Generate short-term wins.
7. Consolidate gains and produce even more change.
8. Institutionalize new approaches in the corporate culture.

A season of starting includes the phases of generating the idea, refining the idea, gaining buy-in from leadership, and making the decision, then recruiting the team to do it, working through the logistics, launching the new thing, working through opposition, and finally celebrating success or learning from failure.

A few years ago, I got our team fired up about on-site venues. We read everything written on the topic at that time and visited Larry Osborne at North Coast Church to learn from the veteran of multisite on-campus venues. We started four venues: Traditions, Video Café, Revolution, and Spanish. Two thrived and two died. We've both celebrated and learned. Part of our learning is that we did not lead the change well with our congregation, in particular with our lay leaders. Our elders and staff were all onboard, but that was not sufficient. I did not help people see the "why" clearly enough—the need and the vision of what could happen. We skipped steps in our hurry to get going. Rather than taking the time to build a leadership team for each service and allowing them to plan out details, my staff planned the details for them, thinking they were helping when in fact they inhibited the lay leadership team from developing ownership. Traditions and Revolution died, but Video Café and Spanish have thrived. If I had paid more attention to the wisdom of others, we may have had more success than we did.

The opposite of "starting" seasons are "ending seasons"—usually not our favorite kind, but very important to handle well. When our Revolution service was coming to an end, the leaders involved did a great job walking everyone through the process. Endings are times of grief for those who do not want it to end. The first response in personal grief is denial, and you see that in closing ministries. Some people can't face the reality that this ministry is coming to an end. After all, they will say, "God used this ministry to change our lives." For some in our church, Revolution was their home, the place where they served for the first time, where they encountered God, and for the first time, belonged.

A good cycle of ending includes plenty of up-front communication. No one likes to be surprised, to show up one day and find that the room is empty with no explanation. Most people prefer to be included in the process to the extent possible. People need to be heard, to be given a chance to say what they are feeling. Often ministries just wind down until they slowly fade away; that's usually more painful. It's better to intentionally end the ministry before its gradual falling apart hurts people and creates disillusionment. We picked a Sunday to be the last Revolution service and let everyone know. We closed it with a bang, one of our highest attendances. We celebrated the people who had served. We honored people who had sacrificed. We acknowledged the pain and did not spin the communication. We threw a party for the volunteers. People need closure.

Transitional seasons combine starting and ending. Leadership transitions exit one person and welcome another. You can view the entire cycle as one transitional ministry season. Some transitions are planned, but many are not. They happen at all levels of the church, from small-group leadership to the senior pastor. Those close to the leader will walk through a season of transition. If possible, it's great for the exiting leader to bless the incoming leader and hand off the baton in a tangible way. When that hand-off is not possible, transitions can include interim seasons. Some denominations have retired pastors who specialize in serving as "interim" pastors for churches who are between lead pastors. "Interim" seasons have their own cycle, whether they involve an interim leader or a facility.

Restructuring is a similar kind of season. When you restructure an organization, you enter a ministry season of transition for those who are affected. The same holds for restructuring how a ministry functions. Physical restructuring occurs when we renovate a facility. Although not a big deal for new people, the change can be huge for those who lived in the previous facility for decades.

Crisis, when it is big enough, will often generate a season. In the world of the church, the crisis can be legal, financial, moral, or doctrinal. Factions arise over power, personality, and theology. Sometimes crisis comes from outside forces, whether it is fire, theft, or a natural occurrence like a hurricane. In Louisiana and Texas, Hurricanes Katrina and Rita created a season of crisis. Conversely, major changes in a leader's life can create a season for a church. When the lead pastor is diagnosed with malignant cancer, that is going to affect the entire church and could inaugurate a season not just for the pastor but for the whole church.

There's probably no end to the list of specific ministry seasons. Church leaders would save so much time and improve the quality of their ministry if they would recognize seasons and seek wise counsel for them. It may be your first time to encounter a particular season, but many have gone before you and a few have codified their learnings. No need to reinvent wheels that already roll pretty well. At times it is wise to hire a guide to help you navigate your raft down a river he or she has run many times. What indicators could signal that a new season is on the horizon?

COMMONSENSE MARKERS

Many seasons are obvious because we create them ourselves. When you dismiss a pastor or ministry leader, you initiate a transition season that you often know is coming far in advance. We often fail to recognize that we have initiated a season. We treat such changes as events rather than seasons and try to keep everyone and everything going as if nothing had changed or happened. That's foolish.

Discernment is required for unplanned seasons—the waves we did not see coming that can knock us off our feet. The difference between an event and a ministry season is its magnitude. How many people are affected? What's the duration? If it is just a week or so, that's more an event than a season. If it lasts for a few months, that's a season. Consider the depth of impact.

Watch for topics that stay in the church-family conversations over weeks. If everyone in the church is talking about something or if the air seems to go out of the room when the topic comes up, you may have a season to ride out. Pay attention if meetings go off the agenda with lots of time spent on an issue that obviously is important to most of the team. It's unwise to press through ministry seasons as if they are not happening. Usually you cannot push them to go faster; they have a pattern to them, a common cycle. When you try to shortcut it, you suffer for it.

Often someone outside can quickly discern what you are too close to see. I meet monthly with a group of lead pastors in our area. It's frankly life-giving. We don't have an agenda, but one of us often has a situation to talk about. Incredible wisdom has been shared and much pain avoided because we help each other see something. You also want to get wisdom from your own team. Ask your other leaders what they are sensing. Try out your hypothesis of what's happening and get their input. When you see what season you are in, help your other leaders see it too, so you can ride it well together.

A capital campaign is a season. It begins when the leadership makes the decision to raise significant funds, usually for a large capital project such as a new building. A leader must give direction to the campaign and a consultant may be engaged. The primary leader will recruit other leaders to build multiple teams, involving as many people as possible. A financial goal gets determined based on the scope of the project and reasonable faith expectations of the church's annual giving. The pastor will hold one-on-one meetings with larger donors and key leaders, casting vision and asking for lead gifts. For the pastor this is an incredibly intense time of meetings with donors and leaders. For the congregation it's also an intense time of seeking God by faith for how much to give. If you try to lead through a capital campaign season as if nothing has changed, you will hurt yourself. If you try to keep doing all you have normally been doing and hold it all in balance, your body will revolt. If you try to immediately get back to work on all the things you put on hold for the campaign, you will be ineffective. You must rest first, then reengage.

In this capital campaign season and all other ministry seasons and organizational stages, how can you release expectations that don't fit, seize opportunities unique to this stage, and anticipate what's next? In the next three chapters, we will develop three kairos rhythm strategies: release expectations, seize opportunities, and anticipate what's next.

Our fourth case presents a seemingly exciting ministry season that carries dangers leaders can recognize if they think through the rhythm strategies. The vision will more likely be realized if some of the chronos strategies are deployed.

Case Study #4
A Current Pastor Has a Large New Vision

1. Identify your issue or situation.

Bill visualized starting a regional church. The church plant quickly became a megachurch that he has now led for thirteen years. Today he sees a new, expanded vision. His fresh vision is to catalyze a network of rapidly multiplying churches. He is early in the process of casting that vision to his leaders and the church. He is asking them to consider a name change to facilitate more locations and signal a new vision, as well as a capital campaign to fund multiplication.

2. What's the problem?

A new vision may unsettle an existing congregation, threatening the viability of the new vision and also undermining a large regional church.

3. What time is it in your church's life?

Organizational stage: After growing very rapidly, the church plateaued in attendance for a few years and is now growing again, so it is either just entering a mature stage or continuing in a longer growth stage.

Ministry seasons: The church is entering a time of fresh intensity with vision change and what that may entail, including a financial campaign and a name change.

4. Apply kairos rhythm strategies.

Release expectations: The leaders need to release the expectation that everyone will be excited about the new vision. Few may share the intense enthusiasm of those who have dreamed the new vision. Release the thought that the change will come quickly or easily.

Seize opportunities: This change presents an opportunity to reconnect with the lay leaders of the church because there is need for much communication. The pastor also has an opportunity to reconnect with pioneer-type people who founded the church with him, but now may be bored.

Anticipate what's next: New churches will be started.

5. *Apply chronos rhythm strategies.*

Pace your church (frequency and flow): The new vision will require that the pace of the church's ministries be adjusted. All cannot and should not stay the same.

Build mission-enhancing rituals (traditions and habits): A new vision should give birth to new rituals that communicate or enable the new vision. Multiplication will demand many new leaders, so rituals that reward and induce reproduction would make sense.

Oscillate intensity and renewal: High-octane visions cast by visionary leaders drive intensity, so that tendency must be matched by times of renewal.

EXERCISE

As best you can discern right now, in what ministry season or seasons is your church? What seasons lie ahead? Give each one a descriptive title. Then use a line or two to describe features of each season.

Our Church's Current and Coming Ministry Seasons

Title   **Features**

Current ministry season(s)_____

_____

_____

_____

_____

Title   **Features**

Coming ministry season(s)_____

_____

_____

_____

_____

KairosRhythm
Strategies

5

ReleaseExpectations

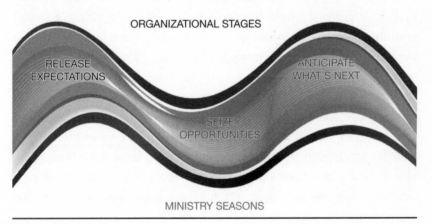

Kairos Rhythm Strategies

It was the fall of 1995 when I first felt God stirring my heart to start a church in McKinney, Texas. At the time, I was on staff with Gene Getz in what was then called Fellowship Bible Church North in Plano, about ten miles due south of McKinney (the church is now Chase Oaks Church). As soon as I settle on an idea, I can see it implemented. All the steps between envisioning and actualizing seem to take too long; my patience runs thin.

Life would have been less stressful for me and my team had I taken the advice we give to young married couples just getting started in their first apartment: Release the expectation that you will have all the stuff your parents have right away. (In fact, you might do well never to accumulate so much, but that's another topic.) Young couples foolishly try to immediately accumulate all the furniture, appliances, and devices that their parents own, and young churches similarly try to imitate on a smaller scale the many ministries of more established churches.

In the beginning days of our new church, I tried to put in place a multiple-staff team to carry out full-orbed ministry with excellence. Looking back, it's obvious that the expectations were insane. Doing it all over again, I would have released more expectations of myself and our team. As a result, we would have had less guilt over what we were not doing well enough. We could have enjoyed ministry more.

Peace comes from living fully in each stage and season without getting sidetracked by resentment for the current season, regret for a stage gone by, or fear of a season yet to come. Having identified your church's organizational stage and your ministry seasons, it's time to ask how to flow well in your kairos rhythms. How can you minister in tune with the rhythms in which you find yourself? Start with releasing expectations.

LIVE FULLY IN THE NOW

Releasing expectations means fully embracing this time and living fully in the time in which God has placed you. In 1 Corinthians 7, Paul says to stay in your condition in view of the current distress. An enduring principle is that we should live fully in the rhythm in which we have been placed, releasing expectations that our lives should be different. Determine to live in this current stage and not attempt to be in any other stage, past or future, or in the stage that another church is experiencing. God has not allowed you to live some other time or place. For better or for worse, this is your moment. This is your time.

Releasing expectations means we accept limitations placed on us by our stage and seasons. For instance, a season of pastoral transition is not the time to create a new vision or launch a major ministry. Often church leaders are frustrated because they want to launch a ministry or make a move that does not fit this time. Let it go. That vision is for another time.

When we release expectations, we refuse to envy a church that is in another stage, cling to a stage we have already left, or ache to live in a season that is yet to come. When I see a great ministry that another church is doing, it's easy to wish I was doing it at my church. If I dwell on it, it becomes envy. Peace is life-giving: "A heart at peace gives life to the body, but envy rots the bones" (Proverbs 14:30). Writing from a Roman prison, the Apostle Paul said, "I have learned to be content whatever the circumstances" (Philippians 4:11). As we practice releasing expectations, we grow in contentment. Peace and contentment come from trusting that we are right where God wants us. We rot our church when we spend our time yearning for a stage or season that does not belong to us.

Older members or founders of a young church may pine for the good old days. Remember when we all knew each other? Remember when I could just walk into the pastor's office? It's not like that now. Releasing expectations means avoiding unhealthy nostalgia, letting go of yesterday. It's great to celebrate the past and cherish fond memories, but don't dwell there. Don't diminish today's diamonds with yesterday's gold.

We feel guilty because we can never complete all the tasks on the to-do list. But not all those tasks fit this organizational stage and ministry season. Start a "stop list" of some of your inappropriate expectations. They are not inappropriate morally or even inappropriate for your church, but they don't fit this time in your church's life cycle. One day, it may be great to start a Stephen's ministry of lay caregivers, but not now. Releasing expectations means giving your church permission to stop doing or trying to do things that are not timely for your stage or season. Is it time at your church for a robust children's choir, a twenty-four-hour prayer ministry, a school of the arts, or a jail ministry? None of these are bad. It may even make sense to do them sometime, but is now the time? Give your team the freedom to say "no."

By trusting that God has you in this season and stage, you increase peace. You trust that God loves his church more than you do. God wants to see the Gospel of Jesus Christ advance more than you do. God knows more than you do. So trust him that with all its difficulties and challenges, God has you in a beautiful season that makes sense on a much larger sheet of music. Let's apply this strategy of releasing expectations to organizational stages and then to ministry seasons.

RELEASING EXPECTATIONS IN ORGANIZATIONAL STAGES

Inception

When a church is at the inception stage, launching, gaining its legs under it in the first years, what false expectations can be released? Much depends on rate of growth. Most churches remain small for many years. Release the false expectation of having the ministry programs of larger churches. A pastor of a church of a few dozen people shared with me that, in addition to preaching and serving as the lead pastor, he was also leading a prayer ministry, the youth on Wednesday nights, a men's ministry, and an outreach program. It was insane—and driving those few dozen people to burnout.

In that early stage, let go of the expectations that you will have systems in place that you expect from more established churches. Let go of unnecessary stress and guilt that you do not have church management software running or that you don't have a newcomer follow-up process. In the early years of your church, just invite all the guests to your house for dinner.

Too many church planters beat themselves up over much that is unnecessary at this stage. Develop a global ministry another day in the next season. You are at the beginning of what we all hope is the long life of this church's fruitful ministry. Your task now is to start it well, not to fully equip it for its lifetime. Release the expectation that your staff of three will have a staff handbook. You have no need for a hiring process or new hire orientation guide. Release the expectation that now is the time to make elaborate plans or write detailed policies. Release yourself and the church. Let it go.

Growth

In the growth stage, you are adding staff and systems, so release the expectation that it will be as informal as it was in the previous stage. For some personalities, it will feel harder to get things done, but processes and systems are required for coordination, alignment, and accountability. Decision making must develop some level of formality— perhaps a signature on a form is needed instead of an okay in a hallway conversation.

For many early staff members, it is hard but essential to release the expectation of relational closeness. In his previous book *The Unity Factor* (2006), and in his new book *Sticky Teams* (2010), Larry Osborne uses sports analogies to illustrate how staff relationships change. At the very start you may be running track all by yourself; it's just you and the track. Then a couple of teammates join you and you are playing golf, all riding in the same golf cart, all playing the same game together at every hole. As the church staff grows, the game changes to basketball; now there are a group of you, but not everyone is on the court at the same time. You are playing the same game, but not the same position. Specialization begins. Finally, you move to football where there are offense, defense, and special teams with their own coaches. Everything changes. If you are on the offense, you may not know the defense's plays or even watch them playing. If the game has changed and you think we're still playing golf, you will be really frustrated. You must release relational expectations, especially in regard to the lead pastor.

A related false expectation is that your ministry position will remain the same. In growing churches, titles and job descriptions must be fluid.

Release an expectation of stability in the growing stage. No longer can every staff member sit at the decision table with the lead pastor. A smaller management or executive team must be created to simplify decision making. If you are in the lead role, it's crucial to communicate well, especially to those who are not invited to be on the team. As a staff member, release the expectation that you will be involved in every decision as you may have been at the start. Your scope of responsibility may increase or decrease as the church grows. Your role may become more specialized or more managerial. Take heart. Your job change may have more to do with the underlying reality of the church's stage than your ability or likability. There can only be so many people around a table.

Maturity

Once the church has reached its maximum size and is at its peak influence, you face different expectations. Release the expectation that change will come quickly. Larger and older organizations are slower to change. Release expectations that the church's culture will change in any dramatic way. By this point, the culture is set and the church is bearing fruit with this particular culture and approach. It can and should have its day. The time for large cultural shifts was an earlier stage and will come again in the next stage. At the mature stage, release expectations of large systemic change. However, if the church is larger, there can be innovation and fairly major changes in subministries, especially during leadership or philosophy transitions. In a mature church, release expectations of informality and spontaneity. Most event planning and budgeting are done far in advance, according to well-honed processes that you would do well to learn.

Decline

When a church enters the stage of decline, yet another set of expectations must be let go. Release the expectation of numerical success as was experienced during the growth and mature stages. At those stages, it's fun to count noses and nickels, and report over and over that you had the largest ever retreat, Easter, women's banquet, or baptism. In the declining stage, release the expectation that you will make those kinds of announcements. Lives will still be changing and healthy ministry can take place, but you are in a different kind of rhythm.

In a declining stage, release the expectation that all the people will be unified and eager to change as is more common in the infancy and growth stages. In decline, people tend to fractionalize and blame. Only a few will see the dangers and the opportunities of this stage. Release the expectation that change will be embraced by the majority who love the way it was and want to bring back the glory days. This stage will not fulfill expectations of welcoming many new guests, building new facilities, or expanding the worship center. Release those expectations for your sake and the sake of the church so you can focus together on how to be faithful to God in this stage. You may be leading the church to dissolve or to reinvent itself as a new church. Release the expectation that it can ever go back to the way it was in the same way that it got there the first time.

You will also experience multiple ministry seasons during each stage. Remember, seasons are shorter patterned cycles. You identified your ministry seasons. Now what does it look like to release expectations in some of those common seasons?

RELEASING EXPECTATIONS IN MINISTRY SEASONS

God is ministering to me right now as I write this chapter. I just opened an email reporting that our giving for last weekend (the last Sunday of the year) was below expectations. With only a few days to go, we are far short of our giving projections—so short that we may be forced to let go some of our friends from our paid staff. That feels incredibly painful. I do not want to face it. I don't want to be in this rhythm. I want to have enough money to launch more ministries and hire additional people to propel the Gospel forward, but that is not where we are. In my view, it would strengthen the church and advance the Gospel to have all the funds we have budgeted, but God must not agree because he has not answered that prayer. So, it's a yes or no question: Do I trust God or not?

Trusting him as best I can, I release the expectation that we can keep everyone on our staff employed in the way they are now. We will likely have to make difficult choices in the next thirty days. A rhythm perspective helps me know that this is merely a season. It will pass. My divine calling is to be faithful in this season, not another one. So I release the expectations that my team will go to a conference, that we can give raises, or that we can increase budgets. I release the expectation that we can hire needed staff, such as someone to help with video. I trust that we are where God wants us to be. (Months later now, we kept everyone on the team but put a hold on 403B matching contributions.)

Capital Campaign

Financial shortfalls can be unexpected, but when you decide to engage in a capital campaign and so do see the season coming, what will you release? If you are the senior pastor, then you release nearly everything not directly related to the campaign. From the moment you begin advance meetings with donors one-on-one to the final celebration service, you are and should be consumed with the campaign. Rhythmic thinking gives you permission to do that. During the campaign, release yourself from every other possible obligation. Get out of meetings you usually attend. Stop going to groups you usually go to. The point is not to live a balanced life during the campaign. These are the play-offs. This is final exam week in college. You do get proper rest, eat well, and engage in basic exercise, but you may need to drop the recreational basketball game. You do not get involved in other initiatives. You back off from community endeavors.

During a capital campaign, it is not time to transition leadership if you can help it. A leadership transition itself is a season. If you must ask a pastor to resign, then you have worked through a difficult time of evaluation and consideration, including multiple challenging conversations. Depending on your governance, you may need to involve the entire congregation in the decision with a vote or involve a judiciary board above the local congregation. Doing it well takes great discernment and focused attention. In this season of confronting a pastor's issues and considering removal, what expectations should you release? This is not the time to launch a new vision. Release expectations of rallying the church to some large ministry initiative.

Pastoral Transition

Once a pastor leaves voluntarily or is removed for cause, the church enters a season of pastoral search. Depending on the circumstances, the search may go forward while the current pastor is still serving. During a season of searching for a new lead pastor, what expectations can you release? You may release expectations such as that your church will grow significantly or that you will write a new mission statement or restructure the staff. You will be interviewing and evaluating candidates, listening to them preach, and talking with references.

When the new pastor arrives, you enter a season of new beginnings. He may have served in several churches before, leading them through various seasons and stages. But he is new to your church. He is at the beginning. What expectations should a church release in a new pastor's first year? Release the expectation that he will know the people or the past history of the church, that he will turn the church around that first year. This is a season of getting settled, of learning the people and the culture. A wise new pastor will wait to make large changes until she has gained trust and developed relationships.

Some seasons affect one ministry more than the whole church. Pastoral transitions in student ministry keenly affect that area, but the impact may be slight on the rest of the church. Thus, each ministry should be mindful of its own seasons, as well as those of the entire church. In student ministry an issue in the local schools can bring on a fresh season.

Crisis and Grief

One year, three McKinney high school students were murdered in one grisly episode. Students were at the wrong place at the wrong time. Our pastors went to the schools to counsel students at the request of the school district. Huge efforts and big rewards went out to find the criminals involved, but leads dried up and dead ends kept the pain alive. Another year, one of our student leaders was killed in a car crash involving a single car and a tree. His mother was on our staff. The funeral for Tyler was massive and powerful. Each of these tragic events set in motion a season of grief for our students. This was a time to release expectations of fun events, silly games, or even doing the next week's curriculum just because that's what was on the plan.

The Community and the Pastor

The rhythms of the community and those of the lead pastor also affect the rhythms of a congregation. If your pastor is in his final years—even if he has been there less than ten years—he will heavily influence the church because of his personal life stage. He is finishing his ministry with a desire to end well, but even if the church is in a growth or mature stage, it is not his time to lead a major new initiative. If your community is going through crisis or upheaval in major transition of ethnic or socioeconomic makeup, then release the expectation that your church will remain homogenous. Is the community in a time of rapid growth or decline? How are the economy, schools, crime in your area?

Our city and county have been growing at rocket speed in the last two decades, so as a church we must release the expectation that school attendance zones will be constant; instead, they are constantly changing. We must release the expectation that those now in power in the political and business communities will be the people of influence tomorrow. In fact, the good ole boys are giving way to the newcomers. We must release the conception that we have a stable population to reach for Christ. We must release the expectation that the current dynamics of our community will be the same ten years from now. So our ministry cannot remain the same, either.

If your church is experiencing crisis or major transition, such as public moral failure or a decision to leave the Episcopal denomination or relocate across town, then your church is catapulted into a season of change. In the midst of the transition, what expectations could you wisely release? Find more peace and contentment by releasing expectations that don't fit this stage and these seasons of your church's life. You can ride kairos rhythms well in stages and seasons not only by releasing expectations but also by seizing opportunities in those same times. We will consider this strategy next.

Rhythmic thinking applies even before a church begins. Our fifth case considers leaders and a few people in the prelaunch stage. Here's a great opportunity to start well by seeing church in rhythm from the beginning. There are many expectations to release. I'm sure you can add to my list.

Case Study #5
Prelaunch a Church Plant

1. Identify your issue or situation.

Doug is partnering with an existing church to plant a church in a nearby city. At this point, he is working full-time in the marketplace. About fifteen people attend a weekly Bible study in his home and a few people are giving money for the future church. Weekly services are projected to begin in about fourteen months.

2. What's the problem?

No weekly church services will be held for more than a year, so will a core group wait that long or scatter to other churches?

3. What time is it in your church's life?

Organizational stage: The beginning of the inception stage; the first month of conception, a long way from birth.

Ministry seasons: Developing the vision of what the church will be like.

4. *Apply kairos rhythm strategies.*

Release expectations: Those getting excited about the church plant need to release expectations for it to progress faster than the established time line, including the prospect of Sunday services. We could make a long list of expectations to release for those coming from established churches to a new church plant, from expectations about buildings to size to range of ministries.

Seize opportunities: Now is a great time to establish fundamental vision, philosophy of ministry, core values, and strategy.

Anticipate what's next: Weekly services are coming and when they do, the core group will invest a huge amount of energy into making them happen every single Sunday.

5. *Apply chronos rhythm strategies.*

Pace your church (frequency and flow): Establish a mental model of healthy rhythmic paces for the church life you envision.

Build mission-enhancing rituals (traditions and habits): Based on seizing the opportunity to develop mission, vision, values, and strategy, build mission-enhancing rituals that will carry and embody the culture you want to create. When those values are more than words but enacted concretely, they will take root more deeply in people's souls.

Oscillate intensity and renewal: Plan in advance how you intend to oscillate between intensity and renewal in the five chronos cycles after the church gets going. Look at the year ahead and map out times of intensity and renewal during your launch year so that you are rested when the weekly services begin.

✌ EXERCISE

Refine your description of your stage and seasons.

1. In what stage is your church? In what seasons are you ministering? How would you modify your earlier description?

2. Based on the time it is in your church, what expectations could and should you release?

3. How can you communicate your answer to question 2 to a wider
circle of leaders and members in your church so they too can get
rid of excess stress and guilt by releasing false expectations?

	Organizational Stage	Ministry Season(s)
Title of stage and season		
Expectations to release		

6

SeizeOpportunities

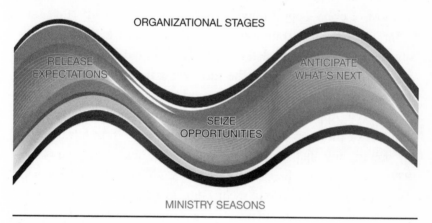

ORGANIZATIONAL STAGES

RELEASE
EXPECTATIONS

ANTICIPATE
WHAT'S NEXT

SEIZE
OPPORTUNITIES

MINISTRY SEASONS

Kairos Rhythm Strategies

My patron saint for seizing opportunities is the young Jewish girl Esther. Her uncle Mordecai challenged her that God had put her in a particular kairos season "for such a time as this" (Esther 4:4). He was not referring to the day of the month or hour of the day but to the unique kairos moment generated by Haman's cruel intent to destroy the Jewish people and Esther's unique role as their queen. In the darkest times we can find the greatest opportunities.

Be alert for Esther-like "for-such-a-time-as-this" kind of moments. If we're trying to keep everything "balanced," we may miss the kairos opportunities that come our way. Seize with gusto what God has put before you right now. Each season carries with it distinct benefits. We waste our lives when we fixate on the difficulties, neglecting to seize the opportunities and enjoy the blessings of a given season.

BENEFITS OF SEIZING OPPORTUNITIES

The Apostle Paul coached the Ephesian church with this challenge: "Be very careful, then, how you live—not as unwise but as wise, making the most of every opportunity, because the days are evil" (Ephesians 5:15). "Opportunity" translates to the Greek word kairos. The New King James Version translates the phrase as "redeem the time." It's an economic term reflecting the idea of taking advantage of a great business opportunity to buy a commodity at a great price. A Greek lexicon says: "Appropriately expresses choice in perilous times... make the most of the time or opportunity in the sense 'take advantage of any opportunity that comes your way'" (Balz and Schneider, 1990–1993). According to the *Complete Word Study of the New Testament*, "The word generally means to buy up, to buy all that is anywhere to be bought, and not to allow the suitable moment to pass by unheeded but to make it one's own." In a definitive study of the word, R. M. Pope defines the force of the verb as "an intensive buying, a buying which exhausts the possibilities available" (1910–1911, pp. 552–554). Wise leaders exploit kairos times for maximum Kingdom impact.

Since we do not know when the Master is returning, today we invest our God-given resources to make the highest return for Christ's mission. As stewards of local churches, we must aim higher than merely burying our resources in the ground. Our call is not to conserve the church's resources, but to invest them well so that when the Leader of the church returns, he will be pleased. None of us knows what tomorrow holds (James 4:12–17), so James tells us to do the good we know to do (4:17). When you pull your resources together to seize a divine opportunity, you can make 100-X impact (Matthew 13:18–23).

When we are young, we enjoy the freshness of each experience for the first time. In later years, we can enjoy experiences more deeply because of how they echo with emotion and meaning from times before. However, when you are racing through ministry, you rarely stop to appreciate the blessings of this time. Seizing opportunities means embracing the joy of the moment. Paul captures this point in Philippians. We can consider it all joy no matter what stage or season we are experiencing. Rather than feeling exhausted from trying to seize opportunities that do not fit the current season, we can find fulfillment and joy when we seize opportunities and embrace blessings unique to this rhythm of our church's life.

In 1 Corinthians 7, Paul counseled single people to delight in their singleness. This is a unique stage of life. Singlehood can and should be a time of undistracted devotion to the Lord. A single person does not have a spouse competing for time and attention. So singleness carries huge Kingdom opportunities to seize for Christ. But many single people miss the joy because they are consumed with what they think they are missing. They long for another season rather than enjoying the benefits of this one. In a similar way, we rob ourselves of joy by bemoaning the drawbacks of the church's current season rather than relishing the blessings inherent in this time. So how do we recognize when a good opportunity rather than a dangerous distraction is before us? How do we know if the "opportunity" is golden or rotten?

DISCERNING FITTING OPPORTUNITIES

Solomon remarked that God has made everything "beautiful" in its time (Ecclesiastes 3:11). That Hebrew word could also be translated as appropriate, suitable, or fitting. Not all seeming "opportunities" are fitting. Some are not divine appointments, but devilish aberrations. How can we discern the difference? Discernment is a gift not universally or equally shared. Most discernment conversations focus on gaining insight into people, but a leader also needs corporate discernment. To see opportunities, you need insight into the organization and the community. How difficult was it for you to see your organizational stage and ministry seasons? You can get better at discernment; it's a skill as well as a gift. Listening is key. Are you listening to what people are saying and not saying? Sometimes an outsider can hear things you don't hear by creating focus groups and surveys. It may be counterintuitive, but sometimes looking back can help you look forward. Over the last year or two, what were your unexpected successes? How could you build on those or seize a similar opportunity?

We need to search our motives for being drawn to a supposed opportunity. Do we have any vested interest? Could this opportunity put us in a good light in a way that feeds our pride? For whose sake are we really considering this opportunity? God has shaped us with different personalities. Some are quite risk-averse. If that's you, then you are usually sure we should pass up this opportunity. You love sayings such as "If it's not broken, don't fix it," and "If it looks to be good to be true, it is." Others are risk-addicted. If that's you, your favorite saying is, "Nothing ventured, nothing gained." Before the church has finished prototyping the last innovation, you are ready for the next one, already bored with the status quo. Churches need both kinds of people on the leadership team. Are you periodically taking significant time alone with God? Discernment is spiritual. The Holy Spirit can give you insight into your church and community, but it is hard to hear the Spirit in the noise of ministry. Are you asking the Spirit to give you discernment to see opportunities? Born in British Columbia, Dr. Henry Blackaby has devoted his lifetime to ministry. He served as president of Canadian Baptist Theological College for seven years and was president of the Canadian Southern Baptist Conference. In his famous study, *Experiencing God*, Blackaby popularized the wise principle that we should not be asking God to bless our plans, but that we should give ourselves to what he is already blessing. In other words, we want to follow God, not ask him to follow us. We preach that people should pray about decisions, but how often have you stopped a church meeting in the middle of a discussion to pray? Did you simply throw up a quick "Help us God!" or did you spend time wrestling with God in prayer? Have you been quiet before God long enough to hear from him? Unless we get away alone for extended time, it can be hard to hear God's voice, to distinguish it from our own voice and the voices of others.

Churches set goals and develop strategic plans. Sometimes we can see opportunities far enough out that we include them in our plan. But what do you do when the opportunity is not foreseen and so is not in the plan? How do you balance setting goals with seizing opportunities? With the future so uncertain and the pace of change so rapid, many advocate preparation over planning. Plans seem to make sense only in shorter and shorter windows of time. Three- and ten-year plans almost never match reality when we get there. During World War II, the famous German military strategist Field Marshall Helmuth von Moltke the Elder wrote that no plan survives first contact with the enemy. His point was that while we plan, we must also adjust. Sometimes you should hold to your plan and pass on the supposed great opportunity; other times you should alter the plan to seize it. How do you know when to do which?

Ask what's at stake. Be sure you understand the opportunity as thoroughly as possible. What does it involve and what will it entail? Economist Henry Hazlitt ([1916] 1920]) wrote, "A problem properly stated is a problem partly solved" (p. 17). Develop a process in advance for how you will handle big opportunities. Who will make the decision? On what basis will the decision be made? My staff has experienced considerable frustration when we change plans we labored to create just because someone learned about a great new idea. When you consider opportunities, it's important to know who is empowered to decide whether or not to seize the opportunity.

In evaluating apparent opportunities, we often overlook the most important factors. We teach that decisions should be Bible-based, but when we encounter opportunities how often do we open the Bible and ask what biblical principles might apply? Any opportunity worth pursuing should advance the cause of Christ. Will this opportunity advance the Gospel better than the current plan and better than any other opportunities we could pursue? Count the opportunity cost. Take time to write down your point of view. What are your reasons to seize it or bypass it? Then bring your response to a team of leaders.

Decisions for the community of faith are best made in a community of leaders because they have a *sensus communis*—an ability to discern as a group what they could not sense individually. The Holy Spirit moves in a mysterious way in the interchange among a group of Spirit-filled church leaders seeking Christ's good. Submit your opinions to the greater wisdom of the team. When the majority—or better, entirety—of the team senses that God is in this opportunity, then move on it with confidence. However, expect opposition. Rarely are all the leaders onboard with any direction. And yet, do not be satisfied with running forward with your small group of zealots. Look back and be sure most of the leaders are behind you. Give people time to process.

SEIZING OPPORTUNITIES IN ORGANIZATIONAL STAGES

As we did with releasing expectations, let's apply the strategy of seizing opportunities to organizational stages and to common ministry seasons. What unique opportunities are latent in each organizational stage?

Inception

In the early years you have the best opportunity to establish culture, mission, vision, and values. Seize the opportunity when people are more open than they will ever be again. When a church is smaller, leaders have relational opportunities that do not exist after the church grows. Enjoy sitting together at the same table in a restaurant, the intimacy you can share with your team, the closeness of relationships. Later, just because of sheer size, you will not be able to enjoy that same close bond with every staff member. Enjoy "playing golf" together while you have that privilege.

Few of us can remember every vehicle we've owned, but everyone remembers his or her first car. Mine was a very used red Ford Pinto with a white top. My dad and I split the $800 cost. Most people can remember their first apartment, pitiful as it may have been. There is something about "firsts" that matters. In your beginning stage, you have most of your firsts. Seize the opportunity to mark those moments and treasure them. Don't let them go unnoticed in the busyness of weekly services. Celebrate and commemorate your first office, rental space, baptism, wedding, staff member, donation, community service project, retreat, and everything else. We don't celebrate enough. You will never have another first, so seize the firsts.

After eighteen months of prayer and preparation, my church held our first worship service on March 16, 1997. We met in a rented space in Faubion Middle School, one of the oldest schools in the city. Every Sunday, we hauled in the sound equipment and children's gear from trailers we kept in members' driveways. We worked hard and long; that's what it takes to start something. More than a decade later, we look back at that time as a wonderful, special stage. For all its craziness, and for all our exhaustion, it was worth it. But at the time we did not stop to enjoy what was happening. We were too busy looking ahead to where we were going next. We made the common mistake of the young father who is too busy to enjoy his child's infancy. We only get one chance to enjoy the first stage. So, church planters, relish the joys of seeing a church born. Stop long enough to marvel at what God is doing in this first season of the church's life. And don't marvel alone. Help the young church family see the wonder of new life: a church is being born! As God is using you right now to load trailers, hand out programs, set up chairs, and hold babies, know that the church will likely outlive all of you and affect thousands of people you will never know.

Growth

If God allows you to move into a growth stage, you will discover new opportunities. Some of the previous opportunities of the inception stage are now gone. What opportunities are endemic to churches in the growth stage? If beginnings are characterized by "firsts," then the growing stage is a time of "news." You move into a new building. You get new computers as you move into new office space. You begin new systems and processes. Seize the opportunity to choose well. This is a time to learn from others. Go to conferences; visit other churches that are ahead of you. Find the current best-in-class approaches, tools, and curricula. You may work through a rebranding process where you refresh your first logo and website. Enjoy the renewal. Seize the opportunity to set in place systems that will carry you upward in growth.

Now that you are past survival and the church is growing, you can more easily look outward. Of course, you should be externally focused from the beginning, but at the start most of your efforts go to making the basics happen. Look outward to seize larger community impact opportunities that can accelerate your growth as you bless your community in the name of Jesus. If the Hispanic population is growing, launch a Spanish service. Look to focus on a people, group, or place in your community or the world.

Seize the opportunity to reproduce. As living organisms, churches are made to reproduce themselves. Certainly reproduce service times, but go beyond that. If you do not seize the opportunity to plant another church or campus in the growth stage, you may never do it. It's harder in the mature stage and nearly impossible in the declining stage. Now is your time to multiply. Once that impulse is embedded in your culture, you have a chance of continuing to reproduce into the mature stage. As Christian Schwarz says in *Natural Church Development*, "A healthy organism doesn't keep growing indefinitely, but brings forth other organisms, which in their turn also multiply" (1996, p. 124). In the growing years, stretch your church's faith. Seize opportunities to raise funds and build facilities to reach more people for Christ. Challenge the church to step out in faith financially. When you are growing, the momentum motivates people on the sidelines to engage.

Maturity

How do opportunities change at the maturity stage? As a mature church, you have the opportunity to leverage your scale and influence for larger impact. This is the time to look for alliances and affiliations. Lead the other churches in your area to make an impact for Christ together. In our area a citywide prayer effort was originated by a lady on fire for prayer. It took larger churches to rally people, and resources to make it happen.

The maturity stage is fraught with danger because, apart from a new surge forward, the next stage is decline. The church feels on top of the world. You are likely at your largest size in both attendance and budget. Systems are stable. The church is solid with a strong reputation. Ironically, this is a time of great peril because we can't see the decline coming, and once it starts it's hard to arrest. Kevin Ford writes, "As a consultant, I have observed that the greatest resistance to change occurs when a church is at its peak—precisely the point when change is most needed" (2007, p. 161). Now is the time to bring on a new, younger pastor. Now is the time to launch a major new direction for the church.

Under longtime founding pastor Gene Getz, I had a front-row seat to watch how he groomed a successor. The church was at a mature stage and he was in his final lap as senior pastor. It was time to make way for a new beginning. Years in advance he had named his successor, my good friend Jeff Jones. Over a few years, he gradually handed over the reins. When Gene Getz left Fellowship Bible Church North and Jeff took the helm, the church was able to start a new curve forward. With Gene's full support, Jeff led the church into a new growth stage with a new name, Chase Oaks Church, and a new location, a few miles north, on a larger parcel of land. Sadly, this kind of healthy succession process is rare. But it can happen. You can move from maturity back to growth.

Decline

Remember that in the darkest days the light shines the brightest. It is not fun to decline, but there are opportunities to seize. While Paul was locked in a Roman prison, he seized the opportunity to write letters and win guards to Christ. If the church has declined to an alarming point, the opportunity to restart usually presents itself. It takes great courage to reinvent a church. Some leaders try to blow on the remaining embers to fan them back into flame. Others put out the fire and start a new one in the same place. You will usually lose more people and decline further before you begin rebuilding.

A growing movement of mergers and acquisitions is preserving church property for the Kingdom. In this declining stage, you have the opportunity to give your facility to another church and become a campus of a dynamic church that is reaching people for Christ. You may also consider giving your building to a church planter to start a brand new church.

SEIZING OPPORTUNITIES IN MINISTRY SEASONS

No matter what organizational stage you find yourself in, you are continually experiencing ministry seasons. What does it look like to seize opportunities for Christ in common ministry seasons? In the preceding chapter, we practiced the strategy of releasing expectations that do not fit a given season. In those same seasons, look to see what opportunities you can seize that are inherent to that season. Even in difficult seasons, and perhaps especially in trying times, there are huge opportunities for those who have eyes to see.

Capital Campaign

There are plenty of expectations to release during a capital campaign, but there are equally many opportunities to seize. This is a great time to disciple your top donors. You get one-on-one time with them to talk about their walk with Christ as well as the campaign. This is an opportunity to cast vision and explain why the church is engaging in this campaign. Remind people of the Gospel of Jesus Christ and why it's worth giving their life to it. What is your overall mission as a church and why should every person be part of it? Here's an opportunity to increase prayer in the whole church, an opportunity to stretch faith and rely on God. A capital campaign is an appropriate time to challenge how we spend our money, to counter materialism and the idols of our day made of plastic, stone, and synthetic fabrics.

Leadership Change

What opportunities can you seize in seasons of leadership transition? This is a time for seriously considering what kind of leader you want to hire. You can look deeply into what kind of church you are and where you want to gain unified clarity. You have the opportunity to hire an outstanding leader for the future. Each candidate presents a potential opportunity, but it's worth taking every caution to hire well.

Crisis and Opportunity

When Hurricane Katrina hit the Louisiana coast, thousands of evacuees came in our direction. Our church offered to help, but there needed to be coordination and communication. Because of a preexisting relationship with the mayor, a spontaneous conversation at a Wal-Mart led to a meeting at City Hall that included all churches willing to cooperate with the fire department and other municipal entities. Several churches hosted people in their facilities until Wal-Mart converted a building they were leaving into a temporary shelter. We established a distribution center for clothes, bedding, toys, water, and personal care products in a new unused warehouse. Volunteers stepped up and gave over and above. Thousands of people were served; millions of goods given away. God was pleased. His churches came together in the name of Christ. I believe it was this very event that created relationships among the churches that later united together as 3e McKinney, a multichurch effort in our city to show Christ to those in need.

Church Plant

A few years ago, we attempted a church plant in Frisco, a neighboring town to our west. Since our own planting process in McKinney had been successful, we tried to follow the same model for this new one. We quickly ran into problems. The pastor and his "action team" (the leadership team) fell into conflict, but we had no easy means to resolve the issues. When we finally met with key people on their team, the situation was nearly irreparable. Confidence was lost. The leadership team did not feel the pastor had listened to them. When it all blew up that summer, it was messy and painful. The pastor of Frisco Trails wisely resigned and rejoined our team. What would happen to the infant church?

Another church plant in the same town had a similar name. Our plant was Frisco Trails; the other was called Preston Trails. A few people raised the "what-if" opportunity question. What if the two church plants merged? Interestingly, there were complementary strengths and weaknesses. Preston Trails was attracting new believers, but had few leaders or givers. Frisco Trails had leaders and givers, but few new people. Frisco Trails assimilated into Preston Trails, providing the majority of their lay leaders. Once united, the church plant flourished.

Conversations and Change

An amazing opportunity started in conversations with Jeff Warren, a fellow pastor across town at First Baptist Church, and Larry Robinson, the city manager. Over the years, Jeff and I dreamed about doing something together in the city, but nothing ever emerged. Below the surface in both churches, God was kindling new missional heart. Over a lunch Larry told us that he was leaving his position. Although he was interviewing with other cities, he said he loved McKinney and had a heart for the underresourced. Unknown to me, Jeff was also talking with Larry and we both had the thought: What if we combined forces and created something new in our community with Larry at the head?

Jeff and I met with Larry to dream about what could be. It took great faith to consider joining something that did not even exist and had no funding. How do you explain to your wife that you're leaving a city manager position for a dream with two pastors? The more we talked, the more it seemed that God might be in this. Jeff and I each talked with leaders at our respective churches. Our church had already formed a separate 501(3)c nonprofit corporation to bless the underprivileged of our community. However, it was currently being led by a previous staff member and all the board members were from our church. I'll never forget being in my office with Jimmy and his wife Meredith, who led the ministry. Before I told the story, I said, "Jimmy, I am going to ask you something incredibly hard." When I finished sharing the dream of a multichurch organization with Larry as its head, I said, "Jimmy, I am asking you to give away your baby." Amazingly, he looked at Meredith and they nodded. With tears around the table, Jimmy agreed to give away leadership.

Jeff said he was getting green lights from the leaders of First Baptist, just as I was from McKinney Fellowship. We decided not to give co-ownership to the two churches but to give the organization away as a third entity with an equal number of board members from each church. I remember the January meeting with key leaders. We looked at each other, asking, *Are we going to pull the trigger?* We did. Only a few weeks later, we launched the ministry. Jimmy and the entire board resigned after appointing a new board with leaders from both churches. In a quick estimate, we figured it would take $50,000 for the first six months to get started. Each church committed to $25,000 without even being sure where it would come from. A businessman, Bourdon Barfield, stepped up to serve as chairman of the board and give office space to Larry.

What God has done is remarkable. There are over thirty church partners. For the first time, benevolence has been coordinated at Christmas. Thousands of people have been deployed in Jesus' name. Through 3e McKinney, churches are making a much bigger impact in our city than ever before.[1] I'm glad we seized that opportunity.

Charter School

Should we seize the opportunity to lease our building to a charter school? A fellow pastor told me the amazing story of how his church leases to a charter school that emerged from their church. That school now has multiple campuses, including a small one in our city. They operated in a church directly across the street from us, but had outgrown it. The head of the school approached us to bring the school to our much larger campus. It seemed like an awesome opportunity. The school was already up and running. The headmaster of the school used to teach in our Mother's Day Out program. Because tuition is free, we could reach out to many underresourced in our city. We could set up a church-run afterschool program with freedom to share Christ. Financially it was a boon, because in Texas five-sevenths of the rent, utilities, and upkeep are paid by the school since they use the building five days out of seven.

But when we came together for a final decision, the sense was that we should not proceed. We counted the opportunity cost compared to other ventures. Each leader felt a growing sense that God was calling us to multiply beyond our campus, not necessarily to build every square foot our land allowed. In counting the cost, we knew that going forward with the school would take tremendous energy in the first year. I was leaning to saying "yes." But after much prayer and discussion, we passed on this opportunity. It was the gathered team that discerned the greater wisdom of saying "no" at that time.

Citywide Evangelism

One November I received a surprise call from Norm Miller, CEO of Interstate Batteries. He shared his heart to reach our metroplex for Christ. Norm developed a plan with a missions organization (e3 Partners) that came to be called "I Am Second." Norm invited us to be a primary church in our area for "I Am Second." We agreed. Three months later my team approached me with the idea that we should do a full-out, all-church campaign through small groups, sermons, student ministry, and outreach based on "I Am Second." But we already had the spring planned, including prep work for all the sermons.

We gathered our team to talk it through because we had to move fast or not at all. We met with the "I Am Second" team. They agreed to help if we would go forward. We wrestled with changing our plans for the spring or waiting to launch the "I Am Second" series until the fall. After long discussion, our team all agreed we should do it now. One of our main motivations was timing. We knew that Norm Miller had made a three-year commitment to "I Am Second" but recognized how fast trends move in media. We changed gears and grabbed the opportunity. People came to Christ and we tangibly increased the evangelistic temperature of our church. Because we moved fast, we did not prepare our small group leaders as thoroughly as we should have. In retrospect, it damaged our small groups, but overall it was a win for Christ. We still see people being reached for Christ through "I Am Second."

Centuries ago, outside the Athenian stadium, there stood a statue of the Greek god Kairos in a running pose, with one shock of hair sticking straight out of his forehead. Here's the point: We can only seize opportunities when they are coming at us. Once they have passed, they are gone. When we live in rhythm, we make the most of every time, and we anticipate what's next.

Satan never sleeps. In our sixth case study, a church experiences an attack from one of its own leaders against the pastor. Rhythm strategies can help leaders walk through such turbulent seasons in a more healthy way and seize opportunities that may not at first be evident.

Case Study #6
Internal Attack by a Top Leader

1. Identify your issue or situation.

Jose's church has recently surged forward after a building renovation, a move to two services, and an opportunity to purchase a larger property.

However, an additional, experienced pastor has come to the church. He was rapidly given responsibilities to help with the growing church. This new leader has become convinced that Jose, the lead pastor, might not have the best interests of the church at heart. He sincerely believes there are major problems with Jose's leadership. He has detailed them in an extensive letter to the other elders to persuade them of his point of view.

2. What's the problem?

An attack from a close leader with a unique vantage point threatens the pastor's continuance and could split the church or at least its leadership.

3. What time is it in your church's life?

Organizational stage: This church has been well led by Jose for twelve years, although the church itself is much older. It is fully engaged in a new growth stage with tremendous opportunity to keep growing.

Ministry seasons: The attacks by this leader have initiated a season of difficult conflict at the highest level that threatens to halt growth.

4. Apply kairos rhythm strategies.

Release expectations: The elders need to release expectations that Jose can lead major initiatives forward under this attack.

Seize opportunities: This conflict presents opportunities to reaffirm Jose's leadership; to prune leaders who are not onboard; and to model for the congregation how to handle conflict well with truth and grace. Jose has the opportunity to search his own soul at a deep level.

Anticipate what's next: This conflict will end. All conflicts do. A season of unity will be ahead after those who hold opposing views move on.

5. Apply chronos rhythm strategies.

Pace your church (frequency and flow).

Build mission-enhancing rituals (traditions and habits): During the crisis maintain existing rituals for continuity and to build confidence that all is not falling apart.

Oscillate intensity and renewal: Jose will need to be particularly careful about oscillating intensity and renewal during this conflict season. Until it is over he cannot deeply rest, but once it is settled, the elders should grant him significant leave for sabbatical rest.

∞ EXERCISE

Identify a few opportunities your church could seize, and then choose one to grab for Christ. You might also identify a supposed "opportunity" to bypass.

	Organizational Stage	Ministry Season(s)

Title of stage and season
Opportunities to seize

7

AnticipateWhat'sNext

ORGANIZATIONAL STAGES

RELEASE
EXPECTATIONS

ANTICIPATE
WHAT'S NEXT

SEIZE
OPPORTUNITIES

MINISTRY SEASONS

Kairos Rhythm Strategies

H ave you ever felt stuck? A few years ago our fast growth stopped. In nine years, we had grown to about two thousand people attending services on a weekend. Although I said earlier that I did not believe fast growth equals health and that a large church is not necessarily a good church, the truth is that I loved the fast growth and identified myself as the pastor of the fastest-growing church in our city. But when the growth slowed to nearly zero, God forced me to look more deeply into my soul. Was there something wrong with me or with our church? Why would I even think something was wrong if fast growth was not inherently good? I was conflicted, to say the least. In hindsight I know that we were in a seasonal plateau, but back then I had no idea how long it would last and was not finding ways to get us growing again. At times, I was not sure we should even try to grow rapidly.

Nothing stays the same. When you feel stuck in your current organizational stage or ministry season, know that it will not last forever; the next stage is on the horizon. All our ministry seasons and organizational stages are comparatively brief compared with our church's life span. Although we should live fully in the present season of our lives, looking ahead to what's next can give hope. Just ahead there is a new start, a new stage, or a new season—a new leader, a new location, or new programs. When you anticipate what's coming, that anticipation fuels the hope that gives you a better church. When the growth of our church stalled, it was helpful to recognize it as a season and know that it would not last forever. I could look ahead to a change, even though I did not know when that change might come.

GRASPING THE STRATEGY: FUELING HOPE WITH ANTICIPATION

In contrast to our English word *hope* is the biblical concept behind the Greek word *elpis,* which describes a sure, absolute confidence that something is going to happen. Elpis is the confident, joyful expectation of the completion of God's grace in Jesus Christ's return. The kairos rhythm strategy of anticipating what's next is built on a kind of hope that is closer to the biblical elpis than to the English hope. In this life, we cannot be as sure of the future as we are of Jesus' return, but we do know that the future will be different than the past. The prophet Isaiah writes in 40:31

> But those who hope in the Lord
> will renew their strength.

They will soar on wings like eagles;
they will run and not grow weary,
they will walk and not be faint.

Anticipation of what's to come gives you strength for the present season, no matter how boring, painful, or difficult. It is the "God of hope" to whom Paul prays for the Roman Christians that they "may overflow with hope by the power of the Holy Spirit" (Romans 15:13).

Even though a moment's thought tells you otherwise, when we are in the midst of a longer season, it can feel like it will never end. Yet there is light at the end of the tunnel. Let this truth free you from the sense of being trapped and hopeless. Take a longer view to put today's crisis in perspective. Parents of grown children look back at the challenges their kids faced when small and long for the days when the issues were a broken toy or food they hated to eat rather than a broken marriage, bankruptcy, or chronic alcoholism. Toward the later years of life, what seemed so big at the time now seems like not such a big deal. The difference is perspective. Adopt a rhythmic perspective that one season ends and another begins. Whether you love your current situation or hate it, it will pass. Children will grow up. Your church board membership will change. Pastors will come and go. A building will be built and then need to be renovated. Programs and patterns of ministry have their seasons, as do styles of music.

The rhythms of your community will bring change. The current makeup of the population will change. Because of global mobility, your congregation will change through immigration and patterns of migration. Even in a stable region, one generation of people die and a new generation takes their place. Whether your city grows or declines, people move on and move in; it will not be the same. Culture itself is always shifting, and doing so more rapidly today, driven by technological advances and an explosion of knowledge. Picture your community forty years ago. Where were the computers, Internet, cell phones, cable or satellite television, DVDs? You could see movies only in the theater.

Who was in political office? What were the primary issues facing your community? Things change.

All stages and seasons will culminate in the final stage of all history: the new heavens and new earth. Our ultimate hope is the return of Christ who will make all things new. We do our work in anticipation of what God will do in the near future. We can persevere knowing these are temporary seasons. Our role in these seasons is to announce and demonstrate the Kingdom that has come and is coming.

What can you do practically to anticipate what's next? Face the brevity of your current season or stage. I find it helpful to estimate how long this season will last. In our personal lives we raise a teenager for only seven years, even though it may feel much longer than that. Parents feel like they are in the valley of the diapers forever, but babies learn how to do it and the diapers are put away in only a handful of years. For how many years do your children want you to put them to bed or hold them in your lap? Not many. When you consider your whole life span, you only raise children in your home for a quarter to a third of your life.

To see what's ahead, it helps to look backward. We can see history more clearly than we can see the future. What was the last season of your church's life? How long did it last? How was it different from the season you are in now? With that perspective, look ahead. When do you imagine a new season will start, apart from events you cannot predict? Name that season. How long do you imagine it might last? The point here is not accurate prophecy, but to grasp that things don't stay the same for long.

When our church first started services and we were holding them in Faubion Middle School, it was a challenge to say the least. Electricity was inadequate, so we blew fuses often. Windows in the bathrooms did not fully close, so it was chilly in the winter. The janitor was often drunk or hung over. We ended up being in that school for only a year. At the time we could have benefited from realizing more clearly that this would be a short season.

How do you know when things will change? Be alert for transitions, signs of change. Listen for signals that change may be coming. Unrest and questions can disquiet us, but they can also excite us if we realize that these are signals of a new season coming. Prepare yourself and the church for change. Change is hard for nearly everyone, except a few of us crazy people who see change like chocolate: delicious. As a church leader, shepherd people through the challenge of change, even good change.

The power of expectation gives the endurance it takes to keep working hard. When you know that a rest, a break, is right around the corner you can keep going full-out on the task at hand. The awareness that a vacation is coming helps you endure today. In just a few months, you will be on a beach, napping in a lounge chair, with the sea breeze keeping you cool. In a season of intensity, plan a time of rest on the other side. Churches need to be able to anticipate a break. The capital campaign will end. The Bible study season will end. We will take a break. In each ministry area, design in a time of rest that people can anticipate.

As we did with the last two strategies, let's apply the strategy of anticipation to organizational stages and ministry seasons.

ANTICIPATING WHAT'S NEXT IN ORGANIZATIONAL STAGES

It's challenging to apply the anticipation strategy to organizational stages because they last so much longer than ministry seasons. You may not even be part of the same church through more than two of the stages. There is more hope for the future in the early stages than the later. Still, in any stage you can anticipate that another stage is ahead.

Inception

In the beginning stage, anticipation can be especially valuable. Starting a church is really hard, but many of those early difficulties go away as you grow. If you move to a permanent facility, you eliminate the need for weekly setup and teardown. Look forward to that day. You craft your mission and create your orientation process, membership process, and ministry model. Once those are in place, they can be refined and eventually recrafted, but not created from zero. The lead pastor will not continue to do so much himself. Leaders come into place. Systems and processes will mature, as will younger leaders. You begin to learn how to do this thing called church. You acquire better gear and equipment. Processes and systems are established so everything is not started from scratch. It's easier to do things the third and fourth times than it was the first time.

Growth

Many things are changing as you grow in size. You might reorganize annually. Titles change so fast it hardly makes sense to print individual business cards. Churches cycle through a pastoral team, management team, ministry team, and executive pastor. Who is in which office changes as roles shift and new people join the team. For many personalities, this degree of change is crazy-making. But it will not stay this way. Anticipate stability ahead. Most churches do grow into their size. Roles stabilize and last longer. Likely you will build buildings or lease permanent space. You will learn how to hire the right staff and how to manage well.

Twelve years into the process in our church, good people have developed a mature financial system, employee evaluation practices, and a relatively stable organizational structure (we last changed it twenty-one months ago from this writing). Our annual calendar is fairly predictable. Our fiscal year begins July 1; we plan and establish a budget for the following year each spring. No longer are we planning from a blank calendar; we are at a different stage.

At this stage, we need to anticipate what traditions have become sacred cows that should next be burgers on the grill. Earlier we had no sacred cows; they may have been calves, but now they have grown up to be cows. At this stage, we need to consider, as Andy Stanly of North Point Community Church says, what "old couches" we need to throw out even though they are comfortable. Earlier, all our "couches" were new, or at least new to us.

Anticipate not growing. That could sound bad and it did feel bad to me, but it is unnatural and unusual to grow rapidly, year after year, for decades. Usually there are seasons of consolidation, slower growth in attendance, as you catch up to your new size with leadership and systems.

Maturity

When a church is in the mature stage you can anticipate a potential new growth phase. In fact, you must seize the opportunity to proactively create it or you will decline. Change is scary, especially when what you are doing seems to be working and the new direction is unproven. Look past the transition to see a future of reaching the next generation for Christ with a new model and new strategies for a new day.

A common frustration at the mature stage is the lack of institutional change and speed. Younger leaders struggle with the inertia inherent to mature organizations. Anticipate that this will change one day or that you will leave for a new place. Even mature organizations can transform or they will decline and eventually die.

Decline

Every church eventually declines. During this stage you can anticipate a restart, merger, or gifting your church to a church planter who will use your property as a base for a whole new church to advance the Gospel of Christ. The church of Jesus Christ will not die. Your individual church will come to the end of its organizational life cycle, but hopefully you have planted the seeds of many new churches over your life span. Anticipate how your church may become the beginning for a new church.

As in the previous two chapters, we will shift from organizational stages to ministry seasons. It's easier to anticipate what's next in ministry seasons since they are shorter in duration.

ANTICIPATING WHAT'S NEXT IN MINISTRY SEASONS

We've described releasing expectations and seizing opportunities in a capital campaign season. In that same season, anticipate what's next. Know that this intense time will end. In a campaign, you can set a date for the celebration service to announce the total commitments. When that is done, the church needs to breathe and rest, as do you and the leaders of the campaign. This is not the time to launch a new major all-church initiative. Let the church anticipate a more restful time. Personally anticipate where you will go with your wife or kids to relax, rest, and unwind. Use the anticipation of the rest to come to give you strength during the many nights out in a row expending yourself to cast passionate vision. The whole church needs this kind of break. Limit the church calendar immediately before and after a capital campaign.

Building Projects

Usually capital campaigns fund building projects that last much longer than the campaign. It takes about two or three years to design and build a church facility. Nearly every project runs into snags with the city over some code, regulation, or process. Budget overruns are common as unanticipated expenses are uncovered. Thousands of minor decisions must be made along the way, from kinds of doors to colors of bathrooms to light fixtures. It's not easy to name the exact day you will move into a new facility, but as it gets closer you can approximate when it will be. Sadly, it is not uncommon for pastors to resign or be let go soon after a building is completed. One theory is that the leader and the church are exhausted. Another theory is that a new building brings more change than leadership can anticipate. For seasons as common as campaigns and buildings, there are books, articles, and consultants to help you anticipate what's to come.

Following the physical building is the shorter moving-in season, which can take weeks to months, depending on the complexity of sound systems, children's areas, and office setups. After the move-in is a season of opening, often a soft opening for the congregation followed by a grand opening to the public. These are seasons you can anticipate and plan for. You can learn in advance from other churches what these seasons will be like.

False Teaching

But many seasons cannot be put on a calendar. You do not know when tragedy will strike, when a leader will suffer a moral failure, when some false teaching will crop up, but you know it will come one day in church life. Yet each of these seasons has a predictable pattern once it begins. When the season will begin is almost impossible to predict, but once it does, you can anticipate it ending. A lay leader in our church asked if we could host a "Torah class" in our church for those who wanted to learn a little Hebrew and the Jewish background to Christianity. The idea seemed innocent enough. A Christian rabbi came to lead the class. More people attended than I expected. At the end of a semester, it kept going. I began to hear complaints of strange teaching. A few left the class and others became zealots for the course. I smelled trouble, a season of conflict. Eventually, I met with the rabbi to ask some questions. When I found that he was teaching false doctrine along the lines of the Galatian heresy I knew we had a problem. He taught that Christians who really want to please God must keep all the dietary laws and Jewish feasts.

Using the rhythm strategy, I anticipated that we would get though this in a reasonable amount of time. While I prepared myself for a season of difficult conversations, I knew that in a few months it would be behind us. As is common for this kind of ministry season, we did research on the false teaching, wrote a paper on our point of view, and met with key people involved. The rabbi left of his own accord but sent signals that we had kicked him out. He continued the class, but in a new location outside our church. Sure enough, in a short time the matter was behind us.

Sexual Accusation

In a Mother's Day Out program at a friend's church, a worker was accused by parents of being sexually inappropriate with their child. As often happens in this kind of season, gossip ran wild—facts got confused and the truth was distorted for a better story. Lawyers got involved. The church entered a season of crisis. Leaders called special meetings; experts were consulted for advice. Communication was crucial in content and timing. What do we tell to whom, and when? In this case, the church's insurance company became involved. Communication became much more difficult as word spread into the community outside the church. Do you speak to the media? Do you issue a press release? No matter how you handle it, it will pass. Use this knowledge to fuel hope when you are in the tunnel and can't see the light at the end; it is there. Anticipate the calm to come.

We all experience "senioritis" to one degree or another near the end of each life stage. Use the power of hope to focus your attention on ending this season or stage well, knowing a new one is coming. You will likely not set up chairs forever in the elementary school, stay the size you are now, or hold on to your current leaders and programs. The members of your board, team, or committee will change. Anticipation gives birth to hope that sustains energy in the present.

The Story of Our Church

Today I find these insights into organizational life cycles both troubling and helpful. As I write this, my church is in its twelfth year. Although I don't like to say it, we are an adolescent, still figuring out our identity, still a bit unsure of ourselves. We have grown into our body at this point. We grew rapidly but now have leveled out, much like an adolescent. We were awkward and tripped over ourselves, not always following up with people well; there were multiple stops and starts of various ministries and approaches. Now our systems and processes fit us. We are operating more smoothly. We are ready to reproduce.

In earlier stages, we were focused on acquiring rental space and ministering to our landlord (each of the two schools from which we leased space). At the same time, we were working hard on finding land. Today, we are not focused on either of those goals. We have our property and built two buildings. Earlier, we were building systems and developing processes and procedures: how to handle pastoral calls on the weekends; how to structure the chart of accounts; how to get new people into small groups, and so on. Today, most of those systems are in place and simply need to be tweaked. Our auditor commends our financial processes and now suggests refining such processes as recovering from a disaster and clarifying intellectual property rights. Those were not, and should not have been, issues worthy of our attention in the opening years.

At this stage I am asking anew: *What time is it at our church?* I am sensing that it is time to multiply. God has grown us into a healthy organism that needs to reproduce. In addition, as I am about to enter my fifties, I realize it is time for me to focus on the next generation. Until very recently, I considered myself a young leader and was puzzled why I was not getting invited to meetings of other young leaders. In my mind, I was still in my mid-thirties. As is common, the church has aged with me. Those who started the church with me are now twelve years older too—amazing how that happens. At first, we easily reached younger families because the leaders were themselves raising young families. But now we must begin intentional efforts to reach, draw, and set the table for younger leaders.

Personally, I must recognize that the new ideas are coming from the next generation. I may not agree with them, like them, or even understand them. But my new role is to raise the money for them, take the bullets for them, and empower them to execute their God-directed ideas for reaching more people for Jesus. For our church, that will mean creating new forums for young leaders, aiming our hiring process at younger staff, and looking for younger elders to bring on the team. It will mean putting younger leaders on the platform to lead worship and preach. To lift up the next generation, it will mean the previous generation making way for the next generation. That means laying aside musical preferences. It means giving your leadership seat to a younger leader, making room at the table by stepping away from it or moving to a different table.

At this stage, we could consider developing the rest of our property; relocating to a better property or selling some property; capping our size at this location and going multisite; or initiating church planting. These were not issues at earlier stages, and once decided, may not be issues again for another ten or twenty years.

At this stage, we need to once again clarify our identity. We started with a white-hot, clear mission and vision that we talked about all the time. Twelve years later, it has drifted, and we have now become something, whether we like it or not. We have developed a culture, an identity. So like an adolescent, we must look in the mirror and discover who we really are, including what we like and don't like about ourselves. We are not molding our identity to the degree we were in the earliest days of our existence. We can work on fixing some aspects of the church that are not as we wish them to be, but much of our identity is somewhat fixed under this leadership, at this stage. Once we have clarified our identity, that exercise too will not be a focus again for a long time. Instead we will try to instill it, pass it on to new people, and replicate our DNA in new churches and campuses.

As I now edit the material I wrote months ago, our church has just completed an extensive exercise in clarifying our identity. Will Mancini, with Auxano, led us through a powerful process that has resulted in a renewed mission statement, a clear, shared identity that we can express well and a sharpened vision for the future. We are now growing once again. Our new mission is to be "people helping people find and follow Christ." That mission is accomplished as we live in four rhythmic practices: engage God individually, connect in a group, worship in a gathering, and impact others. These practices are depicted in the following napkin drawing. The large X represents our vision to multiply groups and gatherings. The bold freshness of our vision has led to a name change from McKinney Fellowship Bible Church to our new name, Christ Fellowship.

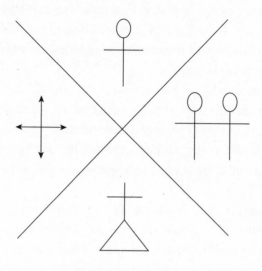

multiplying our mission

In a future stage we will transition to a new pastor. I will leave my position and a new person will assume my role. Hopefully, several years before then, I will begin developing a successor. I will be focused on finishing well and creating the best possible on-ramp for the new leader and his new team. In this next stage that I do not yet see, I imagine we will be asking much more about senior ministry to those and for those who are in their later years.

Only God knows the future, but I am aware that between our current stage and my last lap we will experience other seasons. At forty-nine years of age, I could go on for ten or twenty more years. In the next decade or two, my church might face a split; we might create a network of churches; we might develop multiple campuses. We could transition to a multilingual church with various ethnic services beyond Spanish and English. We may transition to having a "campus pastor" on our original campus while I serve in a broader role overseeing multiple campuses. We might experience huge expansion or painful contraction. God might take me home much sooner or poor health might prevent my continuance as senior pastor. God only knows, but as we encounter each kairos stage, we will ask what expectations we should release. What opportunities we should seize for the Kingdom. And what we can anticipate will likely come next.

Once you identify the kairos waves, you can ride them well with the three kairos rhythm strategies. You coast more peacefully by releasing false expectations that don't fit your current rhythm; you ride with more impact and joy by seizing unique opportunities this kairos season offers you; and you find more hope in anticipating the waves that still lie ahead of you.

Kairos rhythms are complemented by chronos rhythms. Although kairos rhythms are unique and changing, chronos rhythms continue right through the organizational stages and ministry seasons. No matter what stage and season you are experiencing, you will be living them in the five chronos cycles that God designed. The chronos rhythm strategies can empower you to flow well in these cycles.

Anticipation is powerful during dark seasons, but it's also important to anticipate during high-intensity bright seasons of pressing forward. Our seventh case describes such a season.

Case Study #7
Relocation and Name Change

1. Identify your issue or situation.
James recently was handed the baton by his senior pastor in a good succession process where leadership passed from a strong founding pastor to a capable associate pastor over a few years. Now in his new role, James is leading the church to embrace a new culture and reach the next generation. He hopes to lead them to relocate a few miles north and change the name of the church; this will require a large capital campaign to build a new facility.

2. What's the problem?

Too much change too fast threatens James's credibility before the congregation grows to trust him as senior pastor.

3. What time is it in your church's life?

Organizational stage: The church had entered a mature stage, but James is strongly leading the church into what he hopes is a new growth stage.

Ministry season: James has led the church into an intense season of fresh vision, calling church members to embrace great change for the sake of the mission. He calls it "re-planting" the church.

4. Apply kairos rhythm strategies.

Release expectations: The church must release expectations of sameness. The pastor, location, and name are all changing. The new facility will initially have fewer square feet. Not all the ministries will be able to operate in the same ways.

Seize opportunities: The amount of change offers a huge risk, but an incredible opportunity to move the church into a new growth stage with a new culture and fresh vision.

Anticipate what's next: In a few years, given the blessing of God and good leadership, the church will be stabilized in a new location, the new name will be well known, and the rate of change will slow.

5. Apply chronos rhythm strategies.

Pace your church (frequency and flow).

Build mission-enhancing rituals (traditions and habits): Because of the desire to change culture and renew vision, this is a time to change rituals. Some rituals may be renewed or invested with new meaning. External rituals of community engagement can take the church into a missional mindset.

Oscillate intensity and renewal: Those leaders most engaged in the change process as visionaries and implementers of the campaign or the building must carefully oscillate intensity and renewal to avoid burnout or flameout. Once milestones have been met, it will be crucial for key leaders to get significant rest.

✂ EXERCISE

What can you anticipate coming next in your church's life that fuels your hope and endurance today? You could focus on a specific ministry or the whole church.

	Organizational Stage	Ministry Season(s)
Title of stage and season		
What to anticipate coming next		

Chronos Rhythm Strategies

8

PaceYour**Church**

PACE YOUR CHURCH

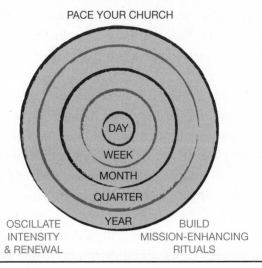

Chronos Rhythm Strategies

Each hour is not the same. The feeling at 3 A.M. is very different from that at 3 P.M. Each day is not the same. Saturdays and Mondays spark entirely different emotions in most of us. Monday is usually a tough day back at the job, which is why people say, "I've got a case of the Mondays." Summer and winter engender different diets from snow cones to soups, and different wardrobes from sweaters to shorts. Similarly, we only frustrate ourselves when we try to lead our churches without regard for the time of year or month. New Year's, Easter, summer breaks, and the start of school each carry their own distinct rhythms. The key to flowing ministry well is to realign ourselves as rhythmic beings in a rhythmic world.

I made a painful mistake the one time I swam in a team triathlon. Never having done it before, I thought it made sense to try to move to the front of the pack of swimmers forming on a boat ramp at the edge of the lake waiting for the starting gun to sound. Let's just say that I was not nearly the fastest swimmer in that Oklahoma triathlon. My pace put me squarely in the bottom half. Within the first several hundred yards of the race, dozens of swimmers literally swam over me, whacking me with flailing arms and kicking feet. I made a pacing mistake that I will never forget. The prospect of drowning seemed very real.

While I am not a runner, I know you can't run a marathon at the same speed you run the 100-meter dash. Your pace varies significantly from an 800-meter race to a mile to a 10K. Each race requires its own distinct pace. If you try to sprint a mile, you will quickly exhaust yourself and collapse. In the same way, each of the five chronos cycles has an inherent pace that can be learned. However, before worrying about the pace of a certain race, we first need to choose which race we are running. That decision will be different for various church activities and processes. Not all ministry runs at the same pace, nor should it.

With tears running down his face, knowing the hardships ahead of him, in his last meeting with the elders of the Ephesian church, Paul used the image of a race to express his passion: "However, I consider my life worth nothing to me, if only I may finish the race and complete the task the Lord Jesus has given me—the task of testifying to the gospel of God's grace" (Acts 20:24). His goal was not just to run well for one stretch of the course, but to complete the race, to finish well. To do that, like Paul, we must learn how to pace our churches. In his first letter to the Corinthians, Paul challenged the believers to run so as to win the prize: "Do you not know that in a race all the runners run, but only one gets the prize? Run in such a way as to get the prize" (1 Corinthians 9:24; see also 2 Timothy 4:7). Using himself as an example, he said he does not "run like a man running aimlessly." Instead he makes his body his slave so that he "will not be disqualified for the prize."[1] How do we avoid running aimlessly in our churches, but instead run so as to win the prize?

Church leaders can advance Christ's mission with more joy by pacing our churches in the five God-designed chronos cycles: year, quarter, month, week, and day. You can figure out how to pace your church by grasping the concept of pacing, identifying appropriate frequencies (cycles) for church activities, and maximizing the flow of each cycle.

WHAT IS PACING?

Novice athletes often fail because they have not yet learned how to pace themselves. Whether racing on bicycles, on foot, or in a swimming pool, those who start the fastest do not always win. Pacing is the technique of spreading out your strength over time so that you do not burn out before the end. An article for runners advises, "When you run within your limits, every workout can be a pleasure. But start even a few seconds per mile too fast, and misery awaits: excess fatigue, loss of motivation, or even injury. That's why it's so important to know what pace is right for you."[2] How might our poor pacing be making the people in our churches miserable with similar problems of fatigue, lack of motivation, and injury?

If we can lead people in healthy paces for specific ministries, we can achieve both greater missional effectiveness and greater joy among those doing the ministry. NCAA All American swimmer and former world-ranked triathlete Bill Ruth says this:

"The most important thing a beginning runner can learn is a sense of pace. Controlling pace is the key to effective training and essential to winning. ... The right race paces use your full potential through the different parts of the race, even if sometimes other runners are passing you, or if you are all by yourself, out in front. It takes discipline, confidence, and experience to hold the paces that get you to the finish having run the best race that you are capable of."[3]

Conceptually, pacing applies to many more fields than just sports. Sara Denning Abbott, a behavioral psychotherapist in New York City with specialization in bipolar disorder and attention deficit disorder, is currently involved in research on pacing as a therapeutic tool. When you suffer with bipolar disorder, you have little control of your rhythms. You swing wildly from one extreme to another; either the accelerator is pushed to the floor or you've run out of gas. Abbott is finding success with pacing as a means of behavioral modification to change neural pathways with time and practice. Her approach uses "pacing" as a tool to gain a sense of control and find ways of living between full out and full stop. This new form of therapy teaches a middle ground focus and moderate pacing.[4] While you may not diagnose your church as bipolar, many of us have experienced wild ministry swings, from intense high-octane moments to utter exhaustion and collapse.

Clinical psychologist Dr. Timothy Sharp deals with chronic pain. He and his associates teach their clients a strategy that, interestingly enough, they call "pacing." They discovered that although this advice sounds relatively simple, it was extremely effective in changing people's lives. His clients reported being able to do activities they had not been able to do before. Having seen the success of "pacing" for people suffering from chronic pain, Sharp and his team are recommending modified versions of pacing for those who are simply busy and stressed. Sharp advises: "Achieving happiness and success in life requires having the energy to do what you want to do. It's hard to be happy if you're literally sick and tired all the time; and the unfortunate reality is that many of us are tired much of the time."[5]

He could have been describing church leaders! Whether you have pain or not, he recommends pacing "to maximize your energy and performance, to get the most out of life and to ensure you're as happy and healthy as you possibly can be." In our churches, we want to help people maximize their impact for Jesus Christ with joy. Pacing is about increasing peace in the process of bearing maximum Kingdom fruit by the Spirit's power.

SETTING APPROPRIATE FREQUENCIES

Doctors are learning more and more about pacing the human heart. Healthy hearts neither race too rapidly nor beat too slowly. Irregular beating is not good either. Increasingly sophisticated pacemakers are surgically implanted to ensure that human hearts maintain a healthy pace. As church leaders, we need to put pacemakers in our ministries so that we run well to the finish for Jesus Christ.

When people feel the constant pressure of all their expectations all the time, they burn out and quit. How many people are streaming out the back door of your church, never to return? Study after study shows a tremendous dropout rate from our churches. And they not only leave your church—they do not even try to find another one. The reasons why Christians give up on church are multiple, but I believe one of the causes is poor pacing. Without proper pacing, we wear people out with excessive guilt and stress, which leads to spiritual burnout.

A consultant recently took our church leadership team through a revealing and persuasive exercise. He asked us to list every ministry, event, study, or opportunity offered to adults in the church twenty-six or more times each year. We thought it would be short list. We were wrong. Granted, some of the opportunities were more narrowly targeted, but we realized we are overwhelming the people of our church. This was our list of frequent ministries:

Worship services

Life groups

Celebrate Recovery

Gender-specific Bible studies

Numerous service opportunities

Care ministries (Divorce Care, Grief Share, and so on)

Shift (for eighteen- to twenty-nine-year-olds)

Prayer meetings (several weekly time slots)

Financial Peace University

When we added the much longer list of less frequent activities, we felt exhausted just looking at it on the whiteboard. I encourage you to make such a list with your own team.

On top of such lists, think of all the good, God-honoring expectations we put on the people of our churches. Church leaders inspire, exhort, and challenge people to give money generously as good stewards, pray fervently with great faith, read their Bibles daily, and write their thoughts in a journal. Then we motivate them: build a great marriage; invest in your children; volunteer in ministries; serve in the community to make a difference and become involved in world missions. We challenge our people to serve in the church by doing their part as members of the body.

Can you imagine a good, loyal church member trying to meet all these noble expectations? Although solutions to this complex problem are multifaceted, a rhythmic approach to church helps address the problem. There is a time for all the ministries listed above and more, but when the appeal is constant and universal, it hampers rather than aids the mission. Rhythm releases volunteers from the unconscious pressure of all our responsibilities coming to bear at one time. You can use the five chronos cycles as a foundational grid for identifying and assigning appropriate frequencies for church activities.

Likely you have prayer warriors in your church who advocate for much more prayer than you have today: "We ought to be praying all the time; have special prayer times; conduct a weekly prayer meeting; and set up a twenty-four-hour prayer team where every hour of the day is covered in prayer." It sounds spiritual and right, but such an approach will rob you of joy because of its constancy. Jesus prayed all night, but not every night.

Bible studies, Wednesday and Sunday night services, and leadership courses can all be questioned, not for their validity, but for their constancy. The treadmill is killing us. For instance, should small groups meet every week, all year? At times we are meeting too often and at times, not enough. How often will you meet as a church board? How often will you celebrate the Lord's Supper and in which contexts? How often will you offer training for your leaders or have a church potluck dinner? How often will you send out an all-church email or newsletter? Answers to these questions change over time, so pacing must be continually reevaluated.

For example, I believe that I have often failed to find a good pace for leadership meetings. In the prelaunch season of planting our church, we formed an "advisory team" that met every Saturday morning for two to three hours. In time, the advisory team morphed into a leadership team of all lay leaders that met monthly. After a few years, the leaders complained that monthly was too often; meetings lagged in their significance and attendance dropped off. We moved from monthly to quarterly, and then at some point, to annually. Leaders lost touch with the overall direction; our unity and momentum suffered. Leaders felt disconnected, even though they appreciated fewer meetings. To be honest, I suspect that the gradual creep of the increasing number and diversity of ministries that were created over the years competed with leader meetings for time and attention.

Misunderstandings and conflict result from lack of clarity about frequency. Coming to a common agreement on frequency helps resolve clashes of expectation. In contemporary churches, the frequency of celebrating the Lord's Supper is a typical issue. Many churches celebrate communion weekly in worship services; other more seeker-type churches have opted not to celebrate communion during weekend services but reserve it for midweek worship gatherings. Some churches celebrate the Lord's Supper on the first Sunday of the month. Others may do it quarterly in services, in a midweek service, or in small groups. Do the people of your church know the frequency you have chosen and why? How often do you do baptisms and baby dedications? Communication of frequency aids unity.

Although people know that meetings are necessary, most of us in churches and on church staffs wish for fewer meetings. In his insightful book *Death by Meeting* (2004) Patrick Lencioni offers helpful wisdom on how to improve the pace of all meetings. His book title indicates the way many people feel about meetings, but, ironically, he advocates more meetings, but of different kinds in various cycles. In diagnosing the problem, Lencioni says that we try to cram too much into one kind of meeting on one cycle. His solution is to vary our frequency according to what we need to accomplish in a meeting. For instance, a daily check-in might be a stand-up fifteen-minute meeting. A weekly tactical might be thirty to sixty minutes. A monthly strategic meeting might take an entire morning. Then a quarterly off-site would likely be an entire day, if not two days, to deal with deeper and longer-range issues.

To consider the pacing of your meetings, list every regular meeting that you are involved in and include the frequency of each. Include every team meeting and one-on-one meeting with staff, members, and those outside the church. My own list was daunting. As a result of this process, I'm currently reevaluating the pacing of my meetings and even whether to discontinue some entirely.

Determining frequency can help break down huge projects and big goals into smaller bites in shorter cycles. In a simple illustration, consider the goal of losing forty pounds. That's not a good daily or weekly or even monthly goal, but it's a fine goal for a year. So if you set that goal, pace yourself in cycles: daily—exercise; fewer desserts; weekly—lose one pound; monthly—lose three to four pounds; and quarterly—lose ten pounds. By the end of year, you will have met your goal. It makes no sense to be frustrated week after week that you have not lost forty pounds. But we beat ourselves up in a similar way when we expect that our church will grow to a certain size or become generous overnight.

MAXIMIZING FLOW

Pacing also relates to the flow of each of the cycles. To *flow* means to move smoothly, with continuity, in a pattern. A day, week, month, quarter, and year each have a flow that can be maximized. Most churches focus on the weekly flow with services on Sunday mornings and a few other set times. But churches can benefit from grasping the natural progression of each cycle. Liturgical churches are historically better at the longer cycles than are most informal churches. First, how you can harness each flow for Christ's mission by bringing the Gospel into the natural flows of your community? School calendars, sports seasons, cultural holidays, business conferences, and community events all play into the rhythms of a region. Second, when are you and your church at your best in each cycle? That may be when you should take on the toughest challenges and make the most movement forward.

At first glance you may think you know the flow of the five cycles; after all, you've lived in them all your life. But most people find that they have given little conscious attention to the flow of the chronos cycles. Time management literature offers rich insight into maximizing your effectiveness in the course of a day and a week but gives less attention to the longer cycles. How does each cycle unfold from beginning to end? This is an especially powerful exercise for an annual cycle. The concept of the church year has ancient roots and contemporary benefits. In the next chapter we will look in more detail at the liturgical year and its potential value for all churches. For now, consider this: What is the typical annual flow of your church life? Whether you are liturgical or not, you have an annual flow, and the older you are, the more established the flow usually is. For example, the church year effectively starts in August for some churches with a back-to-school mentality.

Annual Cycle

August	Ramp up volunteers; welcome-back events for kids
September	Back to Church Sunday; fall series
October	Often a special event or seminar
November	Special holiday service
December	Christmas services and events

January	Start-the-year series; planning cycle begins
February	Special event or seminar, such as marriage retreat
March	Prep for Easter
April	Easter; new series from Easter to Mother's Day
May	Mother's Day and graduations
June	Children and youth events and activities
July	Mission trips and camps

When does your church year really start and end? When are the busy and slow times? The schedule is likely different for various departments or ministries. Our worship arts ministry is very busy just before Christmas while adult education ministries are quite slow.

What about the flow of the other chronos cycles? I find the quarterly flow to be one of the most difficult to discern. Much that we think of in a given quarter is actually part of an annual rhythm. For instance, Thanksgiving always falls in the last quarter of the year, but it is an annual recurring event. We don't celebrate Thanksgiving quarterly. Although plenty of church activities recur quarterly and monthly, there may or may not be a sense of flow to quarters or months in your church context. The point is not to create one, but to be sensitive to how ministry life actually does flow.

In contrast, the week has a very recognizable flow. For teaching pastors, Sunday is the end of the week. Some churches set Monday as a day off; for others Friday makes more sense in order to provide a two-day break. Many leaders have discovered the value of establishing a weekly pattern for greater effectiveness. For instance, Tuesday is a sermon research day. Wednesday is a counseling and meeting day. Thursday may be set aside for strategy and longer planning meetings. Saturday mornings are often a time for periodic leadership meetings, growth seminars, or community service events. Sunday morning is obvious. Although churches have tried worship services at all times on Sunday and all days of the week, Bill Hybel's advice has become accepted: "Create maximum seats at the optimal inviting hour." He is building on the typical weekly and daily rhythms of life in America. Maximize ministry in the flow of life in your cultural context. Our small groups meet nearly every night of the week, but most meet on Saturday or Sunday nights, following common weekly cycles in our area.

The daily cycle tends to be more personal. Few churches have a sense of daily flow as an overall community of people. Monasteries were able to accomplish that with hours of prayer. But if you are not living together in a cloistered community, daily rhythms are more difficult to sustain. Some congregations have tried all praying together at set times during the day, no matter where people are at that time. One pastor in Uganda, Makumbi Johnson, encourages people to pray from 3 to 4 A.M. every day!

Our churches will reach and disciple more people if we lead them rhythmically with good pacing. In order to better reach our communities with the Gospel, we should practice similar kinds of rhythmic discernment about people's cycles in our area. How can we bring the Gospel into the existing natural chronos cycles that already exist in our community?

In times of transition, such as in the next case study, how do you think you could handle the pace of your church?

Case Study #8
Pastor Resigns and Executive Pastor Takes Over

1. Identify your issue or situation.
Daniel went to a church to serve as executive pastor. But shortly after he arrived, the senior pastor gave him more and more responsibilities, and then resigned. The elders asked Daniel to serve as interim senior pastor.

2. What's the problem?
The church's leadership instability threatens its growth.

3. *What time is it in your church's life?*

Organizational stage: This church of about seven hundred in attendance is in a mature stage, feeling quite good about its ministry.

Ministry seasons: They are in a season of pastoral transition.

4. *Apply kairos rhythm strategies.*

Release expectations: The church needs to release expectations of a major move forward until the pastoral leadership question is settled.

Seize opportunities: Leadership can grab the opportunity to redefine what kind of church they want to be. By faith, they can look for a leader who will take them into a new growth phase.

Anticipate what's next: A new leader will assume the role of senior pastor, whether that is the executive pastor or someone hired from the outside.

5. *Apply chronos rhythm strategies.*

Pace your church (frequency and flow): In a time of transition, it's wise to keep the pace consistent for stability. Maintain the frequency and flow of ministries. Leader meetings will increase in frequency for the elders.

Build mission-enhancing rituals (traditions and habits): The same applies to traditions and habits. Rituals sustain credibility and identity in a time of leadership transition.

Oscillate intensity and renewal.

✐ EXERCISES

Identify the frequency of activities in your church. The following list and tables offer examples of how you might analyze your own church.

Frequency of Church Activities
Annually

Christmas Eve services

Denominational conference or its equivalent (Catalyst, Willow Creek Summit)

Mission trip to Africa

Back-to-school blessing of teachers

Setting and approving a budget

Personnel reviews

Camps for kids or students; retreats for men, women, couples,
families
Super Bowl (sports events create opportunities)
Quarterly
Leadership gatherings, trainings
Major sermon series
Taxes, reports, quarterly financial report
Day with God; personal day for each staff member
Monthly
Church social; potluck
Prayer meeting
Budget/finances: monthly close of finances and report
Weekly
Sunday night offering of classes and courses
Celebrate Recovery
Staff meetings
Daily
Time with God in Word and prayer
Opening the facility
Responding to email, blog, twitter, Facebook updates

You can use the following table to describe the pace of various
activities in your church. For instance, in our church we dedicate babies
quarterly.

Activities	Yearly	Quarterly	Monthly	Weekly	Daily
Baby dedication		x			

Identify your church's typical annual flow.

Month	In Our Church or Ministry Area

Identify your typical weekly church flow.

Monday	Tuesday	Wednesday	Thursday	Friday	Saturday	Sunday

9

BuildMission-Enhancing **Rituals**

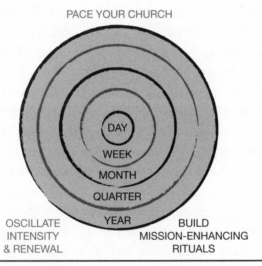

PACE YOUR CHURCH

DAY
WEEK
MONTH
QUARTER
YEAR

OSCILLATE
INTENSITY
& RENEWAL

BUILD
MISSION-ENHANCING
RITUALS

Chronos Rhythm Strategies

Mark "The Bird" Fidrych, a Detroit Tigers pitcher back in the '70s, talked to the ball between pitches. So did the "Mad Hungarian" Al Hrabosky, a hard-throwing reliever with the Cardinals and other teams. Hrabosky would curse the ball, fire it into his glove, and then throw it past hitters. At professional baseball games, before the first ball is thrown out, no matter which team they will be cheering for, the entire crowd stands as one to face the American flag, places their right hand over their heart, and sings the national anthem. All of these are rituals—repeated behaviors that carry meaning for a clear purpose, whether that is to strike out the batter or to engender loyalty to the nation.

Rituals are powerful. They carry values, embody meaning, unify a group, and increase impact. Depending on your background, the word "ritual" carries very different associations. My sons David and Ben and my daughter Melanie think of secret handshakes, songs, and sayings they repeated in their college fraternities and sorority. These organizations create a sense of identity, community, and unity with rituals that all members share, many long after college is past. However, for my son Jimmy, who did not join a fraternity but worked in sports radio, the word looks much different. He pictures athletes' bizarre pregame routines: throwing up before every game, drinking blood, listening to a certain song, wearing specific socks. If you watch basketball players at the free-throw line, each has a unique ritualized set of actions just before shooting the basket.[1] Dribble twice, lick your finger, bend your knees, then shoot. In fact, physiological research has proven that such rituals ensure higher accuracy. When athletes ritualize muscular behavior, their bodies are more likely to repeat the action in the same way each time, thus allowing them to make a higher percentage of shots.

From Buddhism to Christianity to Judaism, religion has always been full of rituals. In hierarchical religious systems, only authorized priests can conduct certain rituals, some of which carry magical power. Other rituals are carried out by all the people of the faith, conveying that we are all part of the community by sharing together in singing songs, repeating creeds, and going on pilgrimages.

In the last few decades of the twentieth century, contemporary informal churches largely rejected traditional rituals because the leaders believed they had lost meaning or become distorted. Although the outer trappings remained, people no longer seemed to connect the ritual with its intended purpose or began to believe the ritual itself had power rather than the reality to which it pointed. Why repeat a creed mindlessly if people are no longer thinking about what they are saying but just going through the motions?

Now in the early twenty-first century, younger churches are recovering the value of ritual. There is something powerful in repeated actions that echo centuries-old patterns and words. Even if some people have lost touch with their meaning, rituals still engrain belief, values, and behaviors. Although a Jewish person may have lost touch with the full meaning of the *Sh'ma* (a classic affirmation of faith from Deuteronomy Chapter Six), the daily repetition implants that truth in his mind, solidifies his identity as Jewish, and keeps him grounded in the Scripture.

Church leaders can advance Christ's mission further by building mission-enhancing rituals into their churches. The God-created five chronos cycles provide a framework in which to develop church rituals. These are natural cycles already built into the fabric of the world and our lives. As a church leader, you can advance the cause of Christ with mission-enhancing rituals by grasping the concept of ritual, establishing traditions in the longer cycles of the year and the quarter, and instilling habits in the shorter cycles of the month, week, and day.

CONCEPT AND VALUE OF RITUALS

In certain contexts, ritual refers to a prescribed order in a religious ceremony. The Ritual *(Rituale Romanum)* is one of the official books of the Roman Catholic Church that describes the ceremonies a priest carries out. But ritual also means "a detailed method or procedure faithfully or regularly followed; or a state or condition characterized by the presence of established procedure or routine."[2] Sociologists define rituals as repeated activities that create meaning in a culture. For instance, according to an anthropology textbook, "Rituals are stylized and usually repetitive acts that take place at a set time and location. They almost always involve the use of symbolic objects, words, and actions."[3]

Sociologist Dr. William Doherty defines three characteristics of ritual. Rituals are social interactions that are repeated, coordinated, and significant.[4] This is the classical, anthropological definition going back to Arnold van Gennep's work in 1908. Rituals may be everyday interactions, or they occur once a year, but they're repeated. They're also coordinated. You have to know what is expected of you in a ritual; you can't have a meal ritual together if you don't know when to show up for it, and you can't dance together if you don't know what kind of dance you are going to do. Rituals are not only repeated and coordinated, they are significant. A ritual is something that has positive emotional meaning to both parties. Doherty's view of ritual involves more than one person. A ritual is repeated, coordinated, and significant. However, other authors use the term to include personal routines that need not be coordinated with others.

For Jim Loehr and Tony Schwartz in their best seller *The Power of Full Engagement*, a ritual can be any healthy routine or repeated action, even if it is performed by an individual. Their research reveals how rituals have enabled top athletes to perform at consistently high levels. Sociologists tend to distinguish routines from rituals based on the assumption that rituals are connected to some deeper meaning or significance. They say positive rituals are "precise, consciously acquired behaviors that become automatic in our lives, fueled by deep purpose" (2003, p. 166). Routines can translate our values into action and embody them. For an athlete the goal is winning and the routine may be as simple as practice makes perfect.

In this sense, rituals are similar to what Stephen Covey (1989) calls *habits*. In a spiritual or business context, we might use the word *disciplines* to describe personal rituals. While these rituals are not part of a shared experience, they are tied to a significant purpose. A ritual must have meaning or purpose; otherwise, it is simply a routine such as getting up at the same time each morning or brushing your teeth.

The important point is that rituals accomplish a greater purpose. In his article for *Executive Update* (2003) Loehr writes, "Positive rituals are consciously acquired habitual forms of behavior that ensure you will do the right thing at the right time with your physical, mental, emotional, and even spiritual energy. Such rituals also ensure that these energies will be there in the right quantity, quality, focus, and force necessary to complete the mission, whether engaging 100 percent with family or providing peak performance for work colleagues."

We want to help the people of our churches engage 100 percent in the mission of Jesus. Rituals can help us do that.

For some people, ritual and tradition are synonymous. Traditions are characteristic patterns, methods, or beliefs passed down over a long period of time. Though distinctions between traditions and rituals can be made, their meanings overlap. Rituals can have little sense of "belief," but the action itself may signify a belief. Rituals that take place at longer frequencies, such as a year, are similar to traditions. In shorter chronos cycles, rituals more closely resemble habits or disciplines. What's compelling to me is the power of rituals to help churches create more and better followers of Jesus Christ.

Rituals have the power to carry values, embody transformation, align a large group, and increase personal impact. Because rituals are so ancient and universal, some people believe they are a way of making contact with our subconscious in powerful ways. Perhaps they touch a fundamental need in human nature. Studies have suggested a neurological connection with rituals.[5]

Rituals enable churches to pass values on to succeeding generations. We see this power in the way repeating the Pledge of Allegiance instills patriotism in children even when they are very young. Singing songs and repeating creeds convey values. Rituals not only communicate values but also actually help accomplish the transformation of those values into behavior. Rituals transfer values from knowledge to life.[6] As Loehr writes in *Executive Update,* "Positive rituals are effective tools that can help you regain control of your life and ensure that you are consciously living a life in support of your personal values and priorities."

For instance, pastors preach on prayer. From those sermons people can understand the importance of prayer. But the ritual of daily prayer when you first awake not only teaches the value of prayer; you are actually praying. Marriage and family websites list dozens of family rituals to enhance relationships. Sharing dinner together is a ritual that accomplishes the goal of uniting a family.

When rituals are communal—something you do with others in a group—they have the power to unify a community. Collective activity reinforces group solidarity. Rituals such as a Memorial Day parade, a Roman Catholic mass, or an annual quilting bee have the power to build communal identity and align a group. A college textbook on rituals notes: "Participating in rituals with others helps people achieve a sense of unity called *communitas* that involves a state of mind in which the usual hierarchical relationships between the members of a group are overcome and individuals perceive themselves as part of a community of equals."[7]

Social scientists advocate rituals that provide family members with a sense of connection to each other. Dr. Doherty advises families how to employ simple rituals to build and maintain family ties. Through hard times, rituals can be the glue that holds families together. Similarly, a compelling article in the American Psychological Association's *Journal of Family Psychology* demonstrates the crucial importance of rituals to the health and well-being of families. Children suffering from psychological disorders can be reconnected to the family through rituals in a way that improves academic achievement and social confidence. Rituals provide stability in times of stress and transition.[8] These same benefits can be experienced in our churches as we employ rituals to align our congregations around the two great commands and Christ's great commission. Much as rituals stabilize families going through turmoil they can also sustain churches through difficult transition, conflict, or crisis.

In addition to communicating values, embodying transformation, and unifying a congregation, rituals can also increase impact for Christ. Loehr and Schwartz correctly point out that rituals must be most rigorous when the challenge is most exacting, such as when soldiers are preparing for war. The United States Marine Corps builds rituals for teenagers to turn them into Marines ready to perform under the most extreme conditions. Young Marines are more effective under fire because rituals have engrained in them proper responses to enemy attacks, dangerous battlefields, and common conflicts with each other.

In "The Human Potential: Rewarding Rituals," Loehr adds examples of pilots and professional athletes, such as Michael Jordan or Pete Sampras. He comments: "You'll notice that any action deemed important has a built-in ritual to ensure that no matter how bad or brutal the conditions, these professionals still do the right thing at the right time. They don't leave it to chance, conscious willpower, or discipline to come up with the right action at that moment."[9]

When individuals try to do something extraordinary, such as winning a gold medal at the Olympics, they follow consistent rituals for years to ensure success under the intense pressure of a global audience. Interestingly, Loehr points out that one long-term power of rituals stems from the fact that they conserve energy. No matter how much we try, we cannot stay concentrated and motivated all the time. Rituals conserve the energy required to will behavior. As Loehr explains: "Instead of relying on willpower and discipline, which can make us feel forced to act, a carefully conceived ritual draws us to action. We don't feel good if we skip it, like going to work without brushing your teeth. The bottom line is that if we want to incorporate new, positive, and long-term behaviors into our lives, we can't expend much energy sustaining them."[10] Loehr refers to extensive research that shows as little as 5 percent of our behaviors are consciously self-directed. It's unrealistic to expect ourselves or our congregations to stay fully engaged for Christ simply out of constant conscious intention. Rather, we can increase engagement for Christ by ritualizing behavior so that we are living for Christ routinely. Where shorter cycles are ideal for habits, longer cycles provide for traditions.

MISSION-ENHANCING TRADITIONS IN THE LONGER CYCLES

Gathering the congregation for a special night of worship, prayer, or training engrains in all of us the value of being together for a shared experience. Annually recurring staff events unite us, forming our sense of being one team, moving together in one direction. After our last time together, one of our staff told me, "I so needed that day. It was great to hear the vision summarized; to talk with each other over a relaxed meal together and to then end the day worshipping together." She said, "I feel renewed."

Liturgical Christians have long benefited from an annual rhythm built into the church year. Whether they use these terms or celebrate on the same day with the same ritual, all Christian traditions recognize Advent, Christmas, Epiphany, Ordinary Time, Lent, Easter, and Pentecost. In her wonderful book *The Circle of Seasons: Meeting God in the Church Year* (2008), Kimberlee Conway Ireton contrasts the value of following the church year with our American cultural calendar:

> Observing the seasons of the church year also helps us embrace the church's telling of time instead of our culture's. Our culture's calendar is grounded in capitalism, which requires consumption. Back-to-school sales, day-after-Thanksgiving sales, the Christmas shopping season, after-Christmas sales, Valentine's Day.... The church year, on the other hand, is grounded in the story of Christ, which is the foundational story of our lives as Christians. It tells the story of our faith—the grand and sweeping story of the God who came to live among us as one of us. [pp. 13–14]

Ireton does a beautiful job of showing how to practically live in the church year by giving examples of many rituals fitting each time, from foods to eat and not eat (Lent) to colors representative of each season. Interestingly, most of the church year is what's called "Ordinary Time." Ireton plays off the word "ordinary," which is rooted in the word "ordinal," meaning to count. This suggests that ordinary time counts or matters. She writes, "Designating the bulk of each liturgical year as 'Ordinary Time' is a profound way of recognizing that the daily, ordinary rhythms of our lives are sacred: that there is something holy to be found in the midst of what often feels like the daily grind" (p. 11). It's in Ordinary Time that the shorter chronos cycles have great power. Weekly and daily rhythms ritualize our faith in Christ.

Our churches have many opportunities to sustain annual rituals that enhance our overall mission. However, if your church is like mine, it tends to value the new over the old, the creative over the repeated, the fresh over the redone. One aspect of the emerging and emergent church movements is a return to liturgy. Some practice this simplistically, such as by lighting more candles, but there is a deeper connection to be found. Our church is an infant in understanding the power of tradition. We're suspicious of it, even as we create our own liturgies and traditions without calling them that. As I write this, a video produced by North Point Church poking fun at contemporary worship services in a hilarious parody is going viral on the Internet. It reveals our contemporary liturgy in all its shallowness and lack of self-awareness.

In an annual cycle, we can also redeem cultural traditions for the Gospel. In Texas, Martin Luther King Day creates opportunities to celebrate diversity and the dream of racial equality, a dream that's part of the Kingdom of God. How powerful this could be if we maintained a consistent pattern of celebration over years and years, engraving the value of the Gospel breaking down barriers among all peoples, God's dream for his church.

Our Hispanic ministry throws an annual party for our community called Fiesta Latina. It happens in September to commemorate the Independence Day shared by many Latin American countries. In our area Latinos hail from many different countries, but they all find a place in this September celebration, which we are redeeming for the Gospel. At a deeper level, we are able to commemorate the independence that God has given us from sin. Through Jesus, God offers to set us all free from our dependence on self and the devil. My hope is that we can continue Fiesta Latina each year so that entire families understand the truth of real independence not from political power but from spiritual oppression.

For many years, we have looked at each new ministry year as a blank slate. During off-site planning retreats, we prayerfully sought God for direction. Our team filled whiteboards and flip charts with ideas. We brainstormed, evaluated, and refined the ideas based on our focus for that year. Now I'm wondering if we were forgetting the power of ritual. Why start with a blank calendar? In newer churches, we often ridicule older churches for doing the same thing "just because we have always done it that way." And there is a point to the criticism; we should not stay with a particular church form of ministry if it's no longer effective. However, in our zeal to be relevant and current, could we be blind to the power of tradition expressed in annual rituals that carry power explicitly in their repetition? The thought of doing that same thing year after year after year could seem monotonous or boring. And yet is that not the very power of ritual—repetition of the same activity to ingrain the meaning?

Perhaps, like us, you have some holiday traditions. On Christmas Eve we have two services: one geared to younger children and one more reverent and reflective. We've had similar elements in the earlier service each year that the children and their parents look forward to: the children shake their parents' keys as we sing "Jingle Bells"; someone reads a children's Christmas book with the beautiful illustrations projected on a screen; we share the Gospel in a child-friendly way. In the second service, we enjoy communion in candlelight. Before writing this chapter, I have to confess that as I looked ahead to the end of this year, my thought was that perhaps we should do something different this year. But revisiting the power of ritual has changed my mind.

In fact, this year we decided not to do a planning exercise based on a blank calendar. Instead, we did the opposite. We took last year's calendar and copied it into the next ministry year. Our opening thought was not to add anything new or different but to do what we did last year better. This was especially true for large missional events in which we serve our community. Both the church family and the community look forward to them. Doing an event one time makes an impact, but when you do it year upon year, the community learns that you are serious about it. For ten years now, each September we've collaborated with our school district and Kohl's department store for an event we call Clothe a Child, in which each child gets $100 worth of new clothes. The power of doing this for a decade far exceeded the power of doing it one time.

Life transitions provide another opportunity to exercise the power of ritual for transmitting Christ's values. Once again, our desire for creativity can hinder the simple power of ritualizing birth, baptism, and graduation. Although these events happen once in an individual's lifetime, the way we commemorate them over and over for different people aligns our congregation around common values. For instance, many years ago I began a ritual during baby dedications of praying for each baby by name and connecting a blessing to a biblical character with a related name. Then the families repeat a vow of dedication as in a wedding, followed by the entire congregation repeating a vow of support for the families. It's the same vow every time. Through this ritual, we are engraining in our people the importance of everyone taking responsibility for the children of the church to raise them in Christ's ways. Similar rituals can be developed for baptisms, high school graduations, and so on.

We can complement annual and quarterly rituals with analogous rituals in the shorter cycles of the month, week, and day. In these cycles, rituals look more like habits than traditions, but they can benefit churches in similar ways to communicate values, embody transformation, align a group, and increase impact for Christ. Informed by her rich background in Orthodox Judaism, Lauren Winner shares spiritual practices (rituals) for Christians that can transform our lives and enrich our churches. She describes traditions tied to life stages such as weddings and aging, as well as habits such as fasting and keeping the sabbath.[11]

MISSION-ENHANCING HABITS IN THE SHORTER CYCLES

Beginning in the centuries just after Christ, and then evolving more fully in the Middle Ages, monastic communities developed daily and weekly rituals of spiritual health. Their lives were structured by prayers according to the hours of the day, rhythms of worship and work, private and communal prayer, and times of meditation.

We do not share communal life in a cloistered community, but many weekly and daily rituals can be encouraged for individuals and families. How powerful for transforming people into the image of Christ if as a church leader you could guide the majority of your church to ritual daily Bible reading. Not reading the Bible would be as unthinkable as not brushing their hair or not taking a shower.

Following the example of Wayne Corderio, Lead Pastor of New Hope Church in Hawaii, a number of churches have created journals to inculcate the ritual of Bible reading and journaling. Most of these approaches have a pattern that each person follows every day. One is SOAP: Read the Scripture. Observe what the text means. Apply the text to your life. Pray to God about what you read. Another is SOS: Study the Scripture. Consider how will you Obey the Word. Finally, determine what will you Share with someone else. The point is to create a ritual that is followed daily and becomes so engrained in people that they don't have to consciously think about it or make the choice to do it. The act has become ritualized.

Such approaches to common Bible-reading plans can be found through history. In the early 1800s, Scottish preacher Robert Murray McCheyne developed a calendar for reading the Bible in a year. He included the unifying power of ritual when he wrote: "The sweet bond of Christian love and unity will be strengthened.... We shall pray over the same promises, mourn over the same confessions, praise God in the same songs and be nourished by the same words of eternal life."[12]

Even though the ritual reading plan is carried out individually, it has an aligning power because we everyone does it.

Our church has shifted from a life journal to a study guide as part of a longer sermon series. The guide offers daily study for five out of seven days each week with commentary on the Scripture and questions to answer. Our ritualized discipleship process is for congregants to first engage the study guide the week before the sermon, then listen to a sermon on the texts they've studied. After the sermon, they participate in a life group to discuss how that Scripture applies to their specific lives. To fuel the groups, we write discussion questions in advance and print the questions in our worship service program. Finally, we ask people to live and share the truth in their daily lives the next week. So the process is study the Word, hear the Word, apply the Word, and share the Word for one common biblical text each week.

STUDY ➡ LISTEN ➡ DISCUSS ➡ SHARE

We've found an incredible increase in life change by focusing our personal reading, sermon, and group study on the same passage or topic. When that focus is shared widely in the church family, the power of alignment accelerates the life change. A unified focus encourages more informal conversation and interaction around what we are all studying. Our recent study through the Book of Revelation provided a powerful example. Each week the whole church read the same section of the book, listened to the sermon, and talked about it in their life groups. Naturally, the questions and issues spilled over into Facebook comments, Starbucks conversations, and family discussions.

You could rally around other daily rituals, such as praying for a certain country whenever it is mentioned in the media, a country to which your church has a special connection and mission. When our area was one of the fastest-growing in the United States, I challenged people to use "For Sale" signs as catalysts for prayer. My charge was, "As soon as you see a For Sale sign go up in a yard near you, begin praying for the people who will live there. Pray every time you see the sign. Then when you see the sign come down, go meet the people for whom you have prayed." In so doing, we were using a ritual to transform behavior to be more like Christ's.

Church worship services provide a weekly ritual to build on. In liturgical churches you already have set rituals, but in nonliturgical contemporary churches few leaders have been intentional about their weekly service rituals. In worship conversations, I hear much more discussion of creativity than ritual. We're good at surprising people with clever dramas, videos, and stage sets tied to current cultural realities, such as a sermon series based on the television show *Lost*. We've geared ourselves to novelty, but can we give our hearts and skills to forming weekly rituals that would engrain the truth and values of Jesus into our congregation?

To establish the value of joy in giving, one church leads the people to clap and cheer when someone says, "It's time for the offering." At a youth camp our students attended, the speaker challenged the students to cheer when he said, "Open your Bibles." Since I was not at the camp, it was unnerving the next Sunday as a group of high school students whooped when I said, "Open your Bibles." For a couple of years, we made a ritual of it and although it sounds a bit goofy, it actually conveyed the value of the Bible. We've had significantly more people bring their Bibles to church, whether paper Bibles or digital ones on smartphones. Some churches are making a video or live testimony a part of every service to uphold the value of transformed lives. Others may highlight a volunteer to signal the value of service or repeat a creed to engrain foundational doctrine.

The point is that rituals carry values. In the last year, we've changed how we end our services. Rather than an upbeat postlude or reprise of the final song, we have shifted to a ministry time with low-key softer music to give people the gift of a quiet few moments to talk with God about what they have just experienced. It has been powerful. I'm not sure how long it will last, but for this season it's been a life-giving ritual for many. At the end of the service we say, "You are welcome to leave, but you are invited to stay. Ask the Spirit of God to seal his truth in your heart."

Many ministries in the church meet on a weekly basis, from rehearsals to Bible studies to prayer meetings. Review your frequency list (see the preceding chapter) for more examples. How could you add value to an existing weekly event by incorporating a ritual that instantiates a core value you want to pervade your church?

The five chronos cycles provide a practical and natural framework on which to build mission-enhancing rituals that advance the cause of Christ in the lives of your church family. Prayerfully consider what traditions you might establish in the longer cycles and habits in the shorter cycles that may unify your church to become more like Christ and help more people find and follow Christ.

Case Study #9
Newly Planted Church in Crisis

1. Identify your issue or situation.

Kevin's recently planted church had only been holding weekly services for a few months when some of his core leaders raised grave concerns about Kevin's preaching and leadership. They felt his sermons were inadequate, that he was not listening to their concerns, and that he was not involving them in leadership decisions but acting on his own. The core leaders met without Kevin to discuss what to do. At this point, it is clear that Kevin has lost their confidence.

2. What's the problem?

Early leadership mistakes dropped confidence to a place where the pastor's continuance had come into question. Such an event this early in the life of the church put the church's continuance also in peril.

3. What time is it in your church's life?

Organizational stage: This church is early in the inception phase.

Ministry seasons: The church is in a serious leadership confidence crisis.

4. Apply kairos rhythm strategies.

Release expectations: The leaders must release the expectation that the current state of affairs can continue.

Seize opportunities: Several very different and drastic opportunities could be seized. The church could release the pastor and hire another person. Or the pastor could release the core leaders and restart the church with new leaders. Finally, the church could go out of existence.

Anticipate what's next: In the midst of a crisis, emotions run high and there seems to be no solution, no light at the end of the tunnel. In fact, this too will end. There will be a resolution.

5. *Apply chronos rhythm strategies.*

Pace your church (frequency and flow).

Build mission-enhancing rituals (traditions and habits): During seasons of significant transition leaders can help people by engaging in rituals that mark the changes. This can be as simple as a going-away party, but can be much more. People need closure. Find ways to mark the endings and beginnings that will take place.

Oscillate intensity and renewal.

∽ EXERCISE

Identify one ritual in one chronos cycle that could enhance Christ's mission in your church or ministry.

	Annual	Quarterly	Monthly	Weekly	Daily
Mission-enhancing rituals to create					

10

OscillateIntensity and**Renewal**

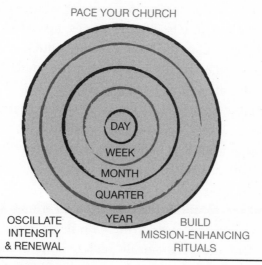

PACE YOUR CHURCH

DAY
WEEK
MONTH
QUARTER
YEAR

OSCILLATE
INTENSITY
& RENEWAL

BUILD
MISSION-ENHANCING
RITUALS

Chronos Rhythm Strategies

O ne of the most difficult, awkward pieces of furniture to move out of a third-story apartment is a long couch with a hideaway bed; it's usually heavier than it looks. You carry your end for a little while and then as your forearms start to give way, you yell, "Let's set it down." After resting your arms for a few minutes, you carry it further, stop to take a break, carry it further, and so on until you get it into the moving van. Your body would not physically allow you to carry it constantly without stopping to rest.

In practical terms, oscillation is the movement between carrying and resting. Without oscillation into rest, our arms would give out and we would drop the couch; but without oscillation into exertion, the couch would never get moved. We need both to accomplish the goal.

Too many church leaders are not oscillating, and neither are their churches. We are neither working hard enough nor resting deeply enough. Two statistics are concerning: the number of pastors dropping out of ministry and the number of churches going out of existence. Although there are times when it makes sense for churches to come to an end and times for pastors to move into the marketplace, many of these moves are not wise healthy transitions, but rather sad cases of burnout or flameout that could have been prevented.

Among those who have not quit, thousands of church leaders report high rates of dissatisfaction. The demanding stresses of church work exhaust the best of leaders. Have you, or any of the church leaders you know, lost the joy of serving Christ? Has working in the church become drudgery? Is it difficult to get up and go fight the fight every day? For those of you who are preaching, are you beginning to dread Sunday mornings? It does not have to be that way.

As consultants to world-class athletes and Fortune 500 executives, Jim Loehr and Tony Schwartz write, "Too much energy expenditure without sufficient recovery eventually leads to burnout and breakdown. (Overuse it and lose it.) Too much recovery without sufficient stress leads to atrophy and weakness. (Use it or lose it.)" The point is not merely that we need rest, but that we need both rest and work, intensity and renewal. Chronic stress without recovery and chronic recovery without stress both serve to reduce capacity. In sports, these conditions are referred to as *overtraining* and *undertraining*.[1] Achieving what they call "full engagement" requires cultivating a dynamic rhythm between the expenditure of energy (stress) and the renewal of energy (recovery) in all dimensions. "Stress isn't bad. Stress all the time is bad.

Downtime isn't a waste of time. Too much downtime is a waste of life," writes Catholic author Matthew Kelly (1999) in his book *The Rhythm of Life.*[2]

Our problem is doing church without oscillation. What's the opposite of oscillation? Linearity. "Linearity is excessive stress without recovery or excessive recovery with insufficient stress." That is not a good life. From their observations, Loehr and Schwartz assert, "Most of us are undertrained physically and spiritually (not enough stress) and overtrained mentally and emotionally (not enough recovery)."[3] Life is not a marathon but rather a series of sprints and rests. If churches try to keep a constant pace, they build up higher and higher levels of stress.

Even man-made machines operate best on duty cycles. We take in our cars for scheduled maintenance. The more miles we drive, the more frequently the oil needs changing, but if we don't drive the vehicle, the oil stagnates. Yet we do not adequately consider our own human duty cycles. Like cars, we need regular work, drive, and intensity as well as rest, renewal, and restoration. According to Loehr and Schwartz, "We become flatliners mentally and emotionally by relentlessly spending energy without sufficient recovery. We become flatliners physically and spiritually by not expending enough energy. Either way, we slowly but inexorably wear down"[4]

Church leaders can advance the Gospel of Jesus Christ more effectively with more joy by oscillating intensity and renewal in the five chronos cycles. We've talked about how to pace church and how to build mission-enhancing rituals in the cycles. To those strategies, we add one last chronos rhythm strategy: oscillating intensity and renewal. This is achieved by grasping the concept and benefits of oscillation, and by employing the strategy in each of the five chronos cycles.

CONCEPTS AND BENEFITS OF OSCILLATION

We're familiar with common examples of oscillation in the physical world, such as the motion of a spring, the back and forth movement of a child on a swing, the motion of a pendulum, and the flow of electrical current in an alternating current (AC) system. Oscillations occur as well in biological systems, and as we will explore, in human organizations.

In oscillation, there is a position of stabile equilibrium and a cycle of movement.[5] Each extreme of the movement is a point of amplitude, as when a child's swing is at its highest point in each direction. In applying the scientific principle of oscillation to church life, I propose an oscillation between the amplitudes of maximum intensity and deep renewal. In each of the chronos cycles, we should normally experience an oscillation between work and rest, intensity and renewal.

The Bible calls us to both Sabbath rest and sacrificial service. God's people are to stop working at times, and we are to work sacrificially at other times. We are to set aside time to rest and we are to take risks for God. We are called to be, at times, both Mary and Martha (see Luke 10:38–42). We sit at Jesus' feet to learn, and we exercise hospitality by "washing feet" to serve (John 13). The point is not that rest and work are to be kept in balance, but that they are to be in rhythm over time. Churches are to fast and to feast, but not at the same time![6]

Jesus says to deny ourselves, leave everything behind, and follow him. And yet, while Jesus says to take up our cross, he also says, "Come to me, all you who are weary and burdened, and I will give you rest" (Matthew 11:28–30). *The Message* (Peterson, 2002) paraphrase puts it this way: "Are you tired? Worn out? Burned out on religion? Come to me. Get away with me and you'll recover your life. I'll show you how to take a real rest. Walk with me and work with me—watch how I do it. Learn the unforced rhythms of grace. I won't lay anything heavy or ill-fitting on you. Keep company with me and you'll learn to live freely and lightly."

How can both be true? How can we take up our cross and also take on an easy yoke? If we understand cross bearing and yoke bearing to be in rhythm in the cycles of life, both make sense. In the scientific language of oscillation, Sabbath and sacrifice are the amplitudes in the cycle.

Jesus' own life was rhythmic. He worked as a single man doing carpentry and masonry. Then, at thirty years of age, he started a three-year itinerant ministry with a growing circle of followers. Some days he worked long hours. Even when his disciples wanted to send the crowds away, he would not. He told the disciples to feed them (Mark 6:37). Other days, he sent the crowds away so he could be alone on a mountain (Matthew 14:23). At least one night, he stayed up all night to pray (Luke 6:12). Other times, he rose before the sun to pray (Mark 1:35). Then, when his "hour" came, he lived the last week of his life fully. Jesus oscillated between times of intensity and times of renewal.

In our churches, we tend to one extreme or the other. We read one set of literature on how to maximize our time, and manage our churches to achieve the highest outcomes. We want to take up our cross; to run so as to win the prize; to be Paul spending himself for the Gospel; to yield the maximum harvest. Then we read a different set of literature on the need for rest and renewal, taking time to be alone, to simply be with Jesus; to be still and know who God is; to be Mary who chose the better part to sit at Jesus' feet. We know either extreme is unwise. We can't sit at Jesus' feet all the time nor can we feed the five thousand all the time, so we often try to solve the dilemma by finding a balance between the two. This is like trying to find the position of stable equilibrium in an oscillation cycle, which is to stop the swing from swinging. You avoid the extremes, but you don't get to swing. The solution is not found in a balance between Sabbath and sacrifice, but in a rhythm from one to the other.

OSCILLATION IN SPORTS TRAINING

Athletes have competed in sports competitions for millennia. Every tribe and nation wants its top competitors to beat those from the other nations. Thus massive efforts go into training. According to David Bourne, the first athletic training manual in Western Civilization was written in Greek by Flavious Philostratus (AD 170–245).[7] In the

Gymnasticus, Philostratus originated a rudimentary form of periodization, or a process of structuring training into phases.

In the second half of the twentieth century, periodization swept the athletic training world. During the 1940s, Russian scientists had success with experiments dividing the training year into different training periods. Their athletes began winning more races in global competitions. The previous approach was to constantly repeat the same workout over and over, pushing to go faster and longer. Other countries took note. The modern meaning of the term "periodization" is largely associated with Tudor Bompa, whose book, *Periodization: Theory and Methodology of Training,* is used by sport scientists, coaches, and athletes around the world. Periodization has become the basis of every serious athlete's training. It involves many variables, including frequency (how "often" you train), duration (how "long" you train per session), volume (how "much" you train in a given week or cycle), and intensity (how "hard" you train at any given time). The goal is to optimize physical performance at the time of the most crucial competition.[8]

Frankel and Kravitz trace periodization to Hans Selye's model, known as the *General Adaptation Syndrome.* "Selye identified a source of biological stress referred to as *eustress,* which denotes beneficial muscular strength and growth, and a distress state, which is stress that can lead to tissue damage, disease, and death."[9] Periodization strategies oscillate the human body from eustress to distress and back again. "Some proven benefits of periodization are improved muscular endurance, strength, power, motor performance, and/or muscle hypertrophy."[10] Could we not imagine parallel spiritual benefits that would come from applying oscillation to church leadership?

THE PRODUCTIVITY OF OSCILLATION

Although at first it might seem counterintuitive, we can accomplish more for Christ through oscillation than through constant ministry. Our effectiveness in seeing more people come to Christ and more people grow to maturity will increase when we practice oscillation between stress and recovery. From the realm of music, Matthew Kelly makes the point that "rests and pauses are as important in great music as the notes themselves. Rests and pauses are as important in great lives as activity."[11] If we oscillate between crescendos and pianissimos, our ministry will sound better and make an impact on more lives.

Not only will our ministry have great impact, but we and our churches will stay in the game longer. Without oscillation, the danger of burnout in exhaustion, dropout in depression, or flameout in moral failure remains high. If we avoid either fully exerting ourselves or fully resting, we will wear down and succumb to stress or boredom. As Loehr and Schwartz say, "To maintain a powerful pulse in our lives, we must learn how to rhythmically spend and renew energy."[12] Churches that prevail for decades make a difference that continues for generations. We want to burn brightly in the darkness for a long time.

Psychologist Mihaly Csikszentmihalyi in his classic book *Flow* (1990), writes, "The best moments usually occur when a person's body or mind is stretched to its limits in a voluntary effort to accomplish something difficult and worthwhile."[13] Relish these times of intensity when you are competing at the highest level, when you push yourself to your limits. It can be exhilarating. Joy comes from the moments of intensity and from the moments of recovery. I've found great joy climbing a mountain, pushing myself to my limit, and I've found great joy lying on a beach, totally relaxed. To reduce stress and increase joy, we need to climb mountains and lie on beaches.

Too many of us don't allow ourselves the joy of maximum exertion or the joy of deep relaxation. We feel guilty when we work hard because we worry we are being workaholics, and we feel guilty when we're resting because we suspect we're being lazy. Oscillation gives us both kinds of joy. "The richest, happiest, and most productive lives are characterized by the ability to fully engage in the challenge at hand, but also to disengage periodically and seek renewal" (Loehr and Schwartz, p. 12). When we lead our churches to oscillate in the chronos cycles, we are more effective for Christ, endure longer in the fight, and discover more joy in the ministry.

OSCILLATE INTENSITY AND RENEWAL
IN EACH OF THE FIVE CYCLES

Oscillation can seem like an abstract concept, but churches can make it practical by applying it to the five chronos cycles. By understanding the flow of each cycle, churches can oscillate between work and rest, exertion and renewal to steward the organizational energy of our congregations. Of course, churches should always love Jesus, but that does not mean constant intensity. There are times to press down on the vision accelerator and times to coast. Are we wearing people out with too much exertion or boring them with too much rest? How can we oscillate a church in each chronos cycle?

By applying the strategy of oscillation to an annual cycle, you can seize opportunities to accomplish something significant as well as seize opportunities to renew deeply. Because you achieve a healthy rhythm over the course of a year, the benefits of oscillation may not be evident in any one particular week, but you can relax about the pressure of "imbalance" in a given week because you know that a time of recovery is ahead. By taking a macro view, the oscillations of an annual cycle give perspective to the micro view of the weekly and daily cycles.

Annually, the Dallas Cowboys oscillate between preseason, regular season, play-off season (they hope), and off-season. In our churches, some of our stress comes from trying to live either in playoff mode or in off-season mode all the time—or worse yet, trying to balance both in every season. In the course of a year, a farmer has planting times, harvest times, and fallow times. In churches, we often want it to be harvest time all the time. Can you imagine a farmer trying to force his crop to be ready for harvest 365 days a year?

Building from your work on pacing, lay out a typical annual cycle in your church. Use a calendar or a simple chart to list each month's activities. In our church, most ministries slow down midsummer (except for the youth), so I take a longer break in June or July. Easter and Christmas are intense times, with extra services and special events. Each September and January, ministries begin a new season of Bible studies and programs for children. We usually launch a new sermon series then too. As the lead pastor, I am fully engaged in September and January. Since discovering rhythm, I've begun taking the entire week off just before Labor Day, as well as the week that includes New Year's Day to be rested for the push ahead.

Here is where the chronos cycles and the kairos seasons can come together. Years follow years with permanent regularity. When you oscillate between work and rest during the year, you can seize the opportunities of both intense performance and personal renewal—and you enjoy both, releasing false expectations that you should rest while you are working and that you should work while you are resting.

How can you arrange the flow of your life and the church ministry by anticipating what will come on an annual basis? Think about when your busy season is. When is it slow? What is the best time of the year for you to start a large new initiative? When might you engage in further education, such as taking a course or going to a seminar? When is a good time of the year to go on a mission trip, take a spiritual retreat, or a study break? Many pastors are discovering that an annual summer study break pays huge dividends. Of course, you also want to correlate your annual flow with your family. If you have school-age children, then spring break becomes an important time to slow down church work so you can give time to your children. Plan how you will oscillate between intensity and renewal.

Studies provide compelling evidence that annual vacations improve health. Using results from a heart study, researchers found that women who took a vacation only once every six years were almost eight times more likely to develop heart disease or have a heart attack than those who took at least two vacations a year. A study found that men who took yearly vacations reduced their overall risk of death by about 20 percent, and their risk of death from heart disease by as much as 30 percent.[14] Other studies indicate that vacations improve marital intimacy, sleep, and mood, as well as decrease physical complaints and fatigue. Are you taking your allotted vacation time? This strategy applies not only to individuals but also to groups and organizations. How will you lead your team to oscillate between work and rest? In the year, when will gather your team to rally them for a push forward and when will you come together to be still and rest in Christ?

Consider creating an "oscillation graph" for your yearly cycle. For each month, circle the number that indicates your level of intensity or renewal from a zero point of average energy expenditure and renewal to a high point of five in either direction with intensity at the top and renewal at the bottom. When do you most intensely expend energy and when are you most fully renewing?

Annual Oscillation Graph

January	February	March	April	May	June	July	August	September	October	November
5	5	5	5	5	5	5	5	5	5	5
4	4	4	4	4	4	4	4	4	4	4
3	3	3	3	3	3	3	3	3	3	3
2	2	2	2	2	2	2	2	2	2	2
1	1	1	1	1	1	1	1	1	1	1
0	0	0	0	0	0	0	0	0	0	0
1	1	1	1	1	1	1	1	1	1	1
2	2	2	2	2	2	2	2	2	2	2
3	3	3	3	3	3	3	3	3	3	3
4	4	4	4	4	4	4	4	4	4	4
5	5	5	5	5	5	5	5	5	5	5

Evaluate your preaching content. How much of your preaching could be characterized as intense, charging people with what God tells them to do, casting vision, and giving prophetic admonishment? Conversely, how many sermons accent what God has given us, how we can rejoice in his gifts, and rest in grace? In a play on Lutheran theology, how is your rhythm between "intense Law" and "renewing Grace"? How we lead in our preaching is one window into the rhythmic health of our congregation.

If you are a communicator, consider your speaking schedule. How many weeks do you speak in a row? In an informal poll of a group of senior pastors, the question was asked, "How many weeks in a row can you maintain high preaching quality before you need a break?" The answers ranged from four to fourteen weeks with the majority in the six to eight range. Very few communicators can speak well through an entire quarter without a break. Some speakers find that a two-week break is much better than a one-week break to really rest and come back raring to go.

In a given quarter, where are you leading your church or ministry? Do you have a vision for this season, this sermon series? If you are merely preaching week after week without clear direction, perhaps you need to give more thought to an intense "press forward" to advance Christ's cause in one specific way or another. Last fall, we led our church through the first five chapters of Romans with the goal that we would come to such a deeper understanding of and appreciation for the Gospel of grace that we would be eager to share it. When a season like that is completed, it is fine to oscillate into another mode. A common mistake is to keep the pressure on after the season is completed. Let it have its time and then bring it to a close. It's not that we ever stop understanding the Gospel, but we do not continue the same intense focus. In another quarter we may move to growing in prayer, or understanding the love of Christ.

How might a healthy oscillation of intensity and renewal play itself out over the cycle of a typical month in your church? A good way to look at the flow of a month is to focus on the weekends, especially Saturdays. Because so many people work Monday through Friday and services are on Sunday, churches offer seminars, conferences, workshops, concerts, and the like on Saturdays. Check your Saturdays each month. Many paid church leaders say Saturday is a day off for them, but how many Saturdays are you engaged in a church event? How many Saturdays are you offering your church an opportunity to come to something? How many Saturdays in a monthly cycle are you performing a wedding, conducting a funeral, or ministering outside your own church? Conversely, consider how many Saturdays you devote to personal renewal.

Many ministry programs run on a weekly cycle. How many weekly services, events, or activities are you offering the people of your church? Recall the list you made of all the weekly recurring activities in your church; it can be overwhelming to the people as well as to the leaders. Some churches have tried reserving a day per week when the church facility is closed. Obviously, church is people and people never stop caring for each and reaching out to lost people. But would it be beneficial to stop church programs for one day a week?

As a church leader, what's your personal weekly cycle? Some years ago, I worked seven days a week on a regular basis. I did not put in a full day on Saturday, but the rest of the days were fairly heavy. My rationale was that I was starting a new church and so much had to happen. Late in the fall one year, the elders strongly encouraged me to take a day off. They were worried I would burn out. On faith I agreed that I would take off every Friday for three months and then evaluate how it was going. The result? I will never go back to working seven days a week. Frankly, I was amazed that by taking one day each week to rest, I actually got more done in the other six days than I had been getting done in seven days. I was more refreshed and sharper because I took time to rest and recuperate on Fridays.

In the cycle of your week, ask yourself: When am I at my best and when do I need to rest? Is there a day of the week where your energy is highest? Tackle the toughest or most important stuff that day. Solve the most complicated problems. Then, when can you best rest? What day will you take off—meaning take time to renew, to do whatever replenishes your energy? As you did on the annual cycle, consider a weekly oscillation audit. How would you graph out your intensity and renewal over a typical week? Circle the number each day that represents your degree of intensity or renewal with intensity at the top of the graph and renewal at the bottom.

Weekly Oscillation Graph

Monday	Tuesday	Wednesday	Thursday	Friday	Saturday	Sunday
5	5	5	5	5	5	5
4	4	4	4	4	4	4
3	3	3	3	3	3	3
2	2	2	2	2	2	2
1	1	1	1	1	1	1
0	0	0	0	0	0	0
1	1	1	1	1	1	1
2	2	2	2	2	2	2
3	3	3	3	3	3	3
4	4	4	4	4	4	4
5	5	5	5	5	5	5

Does your typical week evidence any oscillation? In a typical week, I find that Mondays, Wednesdays, and Sundays are my most intense days; Tuesdays and Thursdays are usually less intense, while Fridays and Saturdays I experience the most renewal. Over the years, I've developed a weekly flow. I schedule team meetings on Mondays, research sermons on Tuesdays, commit my talk to manuscript on Wednesdays, meet with individuals on Thursdays, and take off Fridays and Saturdays. Sundays, of course, are taken up with church services. My best time for longer-range thinking is Thursday and Friday mornings.

Inside a week, is it even possible to oscillate in the short cycle of the day? Absolutely, and it is critical. Recent scientific research has solidified the consensus that circadian rhythms are crucial to healthy functioning not only of humans but of many living organisms. According to *Science Daily*, "New research from Colorado State University shows that the function of all genes in mammals is based on circadian—or daily—rhythms.... The new study presents oscillation as a basic property of all genes in the organism as opposed to special function of some genes as previously believed."[15] Although we have not yet cracked the mystery of how our body maintains an internal daily biological rhythm, we know that if we don't sleep during a twenty-four-hour period, we will pay for it. Oscillation in a daily cycle, and the need for it, may be the most obvious of all the cycles.

Studies consistently show that lack of sleep slows reaction time, decreases concentration, degrades memory, and directly leads to a steady decline in logical reasoning. The average human body needs seven or eight hours of sleep per twenty-four-hour period. Six or less hours triples your risk of a car accident (not enough renewal), but more than nine hours can also harm your health (not enough work). We heal and grow during sleep, which is one of our most important times of recovery. If you are not sleeping well, you will increase your stress and reduce your joy, as well as that of the people around you, because sleep deprivation causes grouchiness.

It is widely known that sleep occurs in cycles of 90 to 120 minutes. Newer research reveals that similar 90- to 120-minute cycles called *ultradian rhythms* operate in our waking lives as well. These cycles help explain the ebb and flow of our energy throughout the day. The human body craves oscillation. You stifle a yawn, stretch, feel hungry, have a hard time concentrating, begin to daydream, make more mistakes—all signs of ebbing energy and all totally normal. It is best to work hard for 90 minutes, then take a short break and go back for another 90-minute focus period. In writing this book, I've tried to implement this oscillation and found it's increased my productivity in pages written (quality is harder to judge!).

As you mapped out your oscillations over a year and a week, you can do the same for a day. When during the day are you at your peak of energy? When do you sag? While you can make adjustments with diet, exercise, and napping to increase your energy and avoid drastic drops, there are daily cycles wired into our physiology that we will not overcome and in fact should not. Rather than fighting them, a rhythm approach flows with them.

The power of living in rhythm comes when we flow with the natural chronos cycles of our bodies and our world. When we try to fight the cycles with stimulants such as coffee, energy drinks, or amphetamines and artificial or medical relaxation aids, we damage ourselves. The attempt to maintain linearity is unnatural and harmful physically, emotionally and spiritually.

By employing the three rhythm strategies in the chronos cycles—pace your church, build mission-enhancing rituals, and oscillate between intensity and renewal—you will advance Christ's mission further with more joy. You will decrease guilt, burnout, and stress while increasing effectiveness and peace. When you live in rhythm, you accomplish more, more peacefully.

Our final case study looks at a church in it last stage. As with churches in the prelaunch stage at the opposite end of the life cycle, rhythmic thinking can be of significant help at the end of a church's life cycle. It can reframe this moment in time.

Case Study #10
A Church on Its Last Legs

1. Identify your issue or situation.

Jim's church has been around for over 150 years. There are a handful of folks left. As a retired pastor, he preaches on Sundays for whatever they can afford to pay him that week. A few faithful volunteers keep the grass mowed and the building clean, but it is getting harder to maintain it all. Guests come infrequently and those who do come rarely return for a second visit. There are no young children.

2. What's the problem?

The church is dying.

3. What time is it in your church's life?

Organizational stage: The church is in the death stage.

Ministry seasons: It is the church's final season, a time of closure.

4. Apply kairos rhythm strategies.

Release expectations: There are many expectations to release and doing so is painful. Release the expectation that the church will continue to exist as it is presently organized.

Seize opportunities: Now is the time to seize the opportunity to seed life into a new church start. The church can gift its facility and property to a church plant or invite a vibrant church to absorb them, opening a new site in their facility. You have the opportunity to see what God has done in the last 150 years extend life to another church by gifting your assets. It's also possible to sell the property and gift the money to another church.

Anticipate what's next: Another church will be housed in your property and reach many for Christ in your community.

5. Apply chronos rhythm strategies.

Pace your church (frequency and flow).

Build mission-enhancing rituals (traditions and habits): Look for rituals of closure to end well.

Oscillate intensity and renewal: There may be a leader you could bless with a renewing vacation to honor him or her for years of dedicated service to the church.

∾ EXERCISE

Identify an oscillation from intensity to renewal in one of the cycles. When will you work hard and when will you rest deeply?

	Annual	Quarterly	Monthly	Weekly	Daily
Oscillations from intensity to renewal					

CONCLUSION

RhythmSolutionProcess forYour**Church**

Kairos	Chronos	Aeon
Waves	Circles	Line
Experienced time	Measured time	Everlasting time
Providence	Creation	Eternity
Ecclesiastes 3	Genesis 1	Revelation 22

Pastors joke that they submit their resignation to God every Monday morning, only to pull it back by the end of the day. How can church leaders stay in the fight, faithful for a lifetime, prevailing in the face of internal attacks and external pressure? The ultimate rhythm of eternity empowers us to press on to the finish line, running strong for the Leader of our churches.

We have focused on earthly kairos and chronos rhythms. Using another Greek term from the New Testament, one day, the eternal *aeon* will overtake chronos and kairos. The Greek term *aeon* can refer to the time to come that never ends; it's often translated as eternity.

Understanding the eternal rhythm motivates us to maximize our effectiveness for Christ in our churches because this life is so brief and eternity is so long. What matters most is what will echo forever. We will be held accountable and rewarded for leading our churches well. Our mission today matters eternally. In Ecclesiastes 3:11, Solomon says, "He has made everything beautiful in its time. He has also set eternity in the hearts of men." "The point is ironic," writes Bible scholar Choon-Leong Seow. "God who has made everything right in its time has also put a sense of timelessness in human hearts."[1]

When we set our eyes on that which transcends our immediate church situations, we can prevail in the battle. This eternal focus motivated Paul to move forward even when his coworkers abandoned him, his enemies falsely accused him, and the Romans imprisoned him. In Philippians 3:14, he says, "I press on toward the goal to win the prize for which God has called me heavenward in Christ Jesus." Moses, in his famous Psalm 90, ruminates on the brevity of life and the eternal nature of God, who is from "everlasting to everlasting." He prays, "Teach us to number our days aright, that we may gain a heart of wisdom" (90:12). In the short time we have here, like Moses we want our work to count and to be as joyful as possible. Leading your church in rhythm empowers you to number your days "aright" so that you lead with a heart of wisdom, establishing church work joyfully in the kairos and chronos rhythms of this world in the light of the aeon rhythm to come.

Focusing on eternity can create joyful anticipation as you realize that the difficult work you are doing today will be rewarded one day. You can share the encouraging hope that "when the Chief Shepherd appears" you will receive "the crown of glory that will never fade away

(1 Peter 5:4). In his article "Pastoring in the Light of Eternity," Larry McCall writes, "It is tempting for the pastor to measure 'success' at the wrong time and by the wrong standard." He points out the powerful temptations and expectations to "produce now." In the context of dealing with being judged by people of his day, Paul said the Lord is his judge. His advice is a great warning for all church leaders, "Therefore judge nothing before the appointed time; wait till the Lord comes" (1 Cor. 4:5). McCall comments, "When I am tempted to 'pass judgment' on whether my ministry is successful or not, I should resist. It is not my place and it is not the right time. Rather than asking, 'How big is my ministry now?' I should be asking, 'How much of my ministry will survive the fire of God's testing on that Great Day?'"[2]

It is the rhythm of eternity that empowers us to be steadfast and immovable, giving ourselves wholeheartedly to the work of the Lord. On the day that Christ returns, we will know that we did not run for nothing (1 Corinthians 15:58; Philippians 2:16) when we hear "well done good and faithful servant" (Matthew 25:21–23).

The mission matters eternally, not just for us on Judgment Day, but also for those to whom we minister. The church carries and embodies the Gospel to the world. We announce that the King has come and is returning. In this in-between time, our churches demonstrate the reality of the Kingdom. We're embassies of the Kingdom of Heaven in which the reign of the King is to be the rule of life. Between the comings of the humble King on the donkey and the warrior King on the white horse, churches disciple the nations. It's the eternal stakes of the mission that motivate us to give our all in the Spirit's power for the advance of the Gospel of Jesus. Why else lead a church?

We can endure difficult days when we remember that ultimate rest is coming. A focus on the ultimate future sustains us today with vivid hope. Understanding the ultimate rhythm can help us release false expectations. In this case, we can—and should—release the erroneous expectation that this life will ever be paradise. Seize opportunities to do that which will last forever. Anticipate eternal joy to come. That is the source of true and rich hope. So in view of the eternal rhythm to come, today we want to flow our ministries as well as possible in the earthly kairos and chronos rhythms.

A RHYTHM SOLUTION PROCESS
FOR CHURCHES

If you are anything like me, you're reading several books at once. Here's the problem: Do I really digest and apply what I've learned from the books I read? Often the answer is "no." So I'm impressed you made it this far into the book, or maybe you jumped to this chapter. In either case, the question is how you can practically apply the rhythm concepts to your church. The simple Rhythm Solution Process for Churches shown at the end of this chapter is a one-page worksheet.[3]

It's valuable to involve a team of leaders in analyzing your situation and creatively determining how rhythm strategies can improve your church. Start with a real-life situation in your church right now. Take the time to really understand the problem. Economist Henry Hazlitt writes, "A problem properly stated is a problem partly solved."[4] Often we race to solutions before we have honestly grasped the problem we are attempting to solve. To the Jewish crowds who questioned Jesus' healing on the Sabbath, Jesus said, "Stop judging by mere appearances, and make a right judgment" (John 7:23–24). Working the issue is the most neglected practice in most decision making. Time taken at the front end to grasp the issue is directly proportional to time at the back end to solve the issue.

After clarifying your issue or problem, the next step is to identify what time it is in your church. In what organizational stage are you and what ministry seasons are you experiencing? Are your stresses related more to a ministry season or to your organizational stage—or both? To apply the rhythm strategies to the current situations in your church, you must identify what time it is. Are you squarely in one of the five major stages (inception and early years, growth, maturity, decline, death) or are you in transition from one to another? In what ministry season or seasons do you find yourself?

Focus on the organizational stage or ministry season that is creating the greatest challenge and then ask strategic kairos questions: What expectations can we release to increase our peace? What opportunities can we seize to advance the Gospel? What can we anticipate, to increase our hope?

Next, move to the chronos strategies. Pace your church: Can you reset the frequency of some church activities? Can you create a better flow within a particular cycle? Build mission-enhancing rituals: What mission-enhancing traditions can you set in longer cycles? What mission-enhancing habits can you establish in shorter cycles? Oscillate between intensity and renewal: Does your church need a shot of intensity or a period of rest? How can you oscillate better in one or more of the five chronos cycles? It is possible to apply all six rhythm strategies to each church situation, but that is typically overkill. Most churches can take only one or two action steps at any given time. Focus on one strategy that helps most right now.

None of us see ourselves clearly. When your problems are long-standing, complex, or difficult to solve, involve a trusted consultant or wise adviser to help. Often, another person can quickly see something you can't see because you are too close to it. The infamous road to hell is proverbially paved with good intentions. Ask your adviser to follow up with you in few weeks. If you will share your rhythm solutions with a wider circle of leaders or even the entire congregation, you will increase the likelihood of making lasting changes.

TAKING IT HOME

The foundational reality of rhythm makes ignoring it foolish. Whether you agree with the six strategies or not, it is undeniable that God made time's flow cyclical. You can leverage insight into the cyclical structure of our temporal experience to advance the cause of Christ. Similarly, it is clear that churches develop over time in stages and are always living through one season or another. Knowing that kairos times come and go, you can lead your church to maximize those times for the Kingdom mission of Jesus Christ.

My hope is that your church helps many more people find and follow Christ. Our mandate is clear: we are to disciple the nations with the authority of the King by witnessing to the world that the King has come and is returning. What time is it in your church? I hope you've decided to ask that question at a deep level. By leading your church in rhythm, you can more effectively carry out Jesus' mission with greater joy.

You can increase your focus in each kairos stage and season by releasing expectations that don't fit that time. By so doing, you will jettison false guilt, reduce excessive stress, and minimize the danger of burnout. You can seize opportunities for Christ that are unique to each kairos time and thus advance the Gospel more rapidly. You can anticipate what's next, knowing that no kairos stage or season lasts forever, filling your church with more intensity in this season and more hope for the one to come. You will avoid wasting resources and instead unify your people for what matters most at this unique time in the life of your church.

With your insight into the five chronos cycles, you can maximize ministry in each cycle while generating more peace and joy in the process. Together with your team, you can discover more sustainable paces for ministry in the most appropriate frequencies. You can learn to flow ministry in each cycle so you bear the most fruit possible. To embed the mission and commands of Christ in your church, you can develop mission-enhancing rituals in the five cycles. These rituals have the power to shape a Christ-centered, Bible-based, Spirit-empowered culture aimed at multiplying disciples and churches to impact your community and touch the ends of the earth. There are times to lead your church full blast and times to drink deeply from the water of life to renew strength for the next battle. Oscillate intensity and renewal in each cycle so you yield a large harvest year after year without wearing out before your time is done.

Some books end with a prescription for action. It's common to list points for how to put the ideas to work or where to go from here. Instead, I encourage you to make your own list. Write your own pre-scription. Take a moment to pray. Ask God to reveal to you by the Spirit what he wants you to take from this book. Then write down what comes to your mind. At the end of the book, I've given you a page to record what God brings to your mind. Use it to crystallize your takeaway as soon as you finish before you forget the insights you gained. What is most applicable to your church right now? Ask God to show that to you. Write down not just a prescription for yourself but also for your church.

What if thousands of church leaders opened their eyes to see the forgotten dimension of seasons and cycles? Too many churches of every shape, size, and flavor are stuck, spinning in circles, wasting the resources and opportunities God has entrusted to them. Although rhythm is not a magic pill that solves all problems, opening the question of timing can dramatically improve your church and the experience of your people. In Philippians, Paul describes ministry as counting everything as loss for the sake of Christ, pressing on for the prize, all the while rejoicing, content in every circumstance, and at peace in Christ. Whether he was personally appointing elders to lead multiplying churches all over the Mediterranean world or he was in prison sharing Christ with Roman guards, Paul maximized every kairos time for Jesus. He released expec-tations, enabling him to know the peace of God, seized opportunities to strive for the faith of the Gospel, anticipated the next time he would see the Philippians, and ultimately longed for the time he would depart and be with Christ. No matter where Paul was, he disciplined himself for godliness. What if our churches were filled with people living like this?

This book offers a first peek into the rich idea of rhythm. My intent has been to kick off conversations and prod thinking. The richness and depth of a rhythm paradigm has yet to be fully tapped. I hope you will further explore implications and benefits of a rhythm paradigm for churches worldwide. Perhaps God will use you to extend and expand the concept of rhythm far beyond what I've done. Experiment and document what you do so you can share it with others. Play with the idea of rhythm and prayerfully discover more powerful and practical ways rhythmic thinking can advance Christ's mission through churches. *Your Church in Rhythm* offers open source code. Build on the ideas to improve and multiply churches so that the Gospel of the Kingdom goes to the whole world, and then the end will come.

✌ EXERCISE

Use the Rhythm Solution Process for Churches to help you address an issue in your church. Remember that while all six rhythm strategies could apply, it's best to focus on only one to three at a time.

Rhythm Solution Process for Churches

1. Identify your issue or situation: What's the problem?

2. What time is it in your church's life?

    Organizational stage:

    Ministry season(s):

3. Apply kairos rhythm strategies.

    Release expectations:

    Seize opportunities:

    Anticipate what's next:

4. Apply chronos rhythm strategies.

    Set your pace (frequency and flow):

    Build rituals (traditions and habits):

    Oscillate intensity and renewal:

My Takeaway
Ask the Holy Spirit to show you the most important insights for you
and for your church. Prayerfully determine the first action you should
take to improve your church and with whom you will first share your
insights.

My top three insights:

1.

2.

3.

My first action step:

The first person with whom I will share my insights:

DISCUSSION**QUESTIONS**

You will find richer wisdom by engaging rhythm as a team than you can by yourself. The chances of improving your church go up dramatically when a team of leaders works through the book together. Read and discuss the book a section at a time. Encourage the group to complete the exercise at the end of each chapter. Give an overview sharing why you think this book has value for your team and your church. The following questions can be helpful in an introductory meeting.

Why are you interested in reading this book?

What questions do you have about the book?

What issues do you hope the book will address?

What objections or concerns do you have even before you've read it?

What do you hope you will get out of it?

INTRODUCTION AND PART 1

Why do you think the notion of a "balanced church" could be dangerous?

What makes rhythm such a powerful idea?

What are the differences between the two kinds of rhythm: chronos and kairos? Give some examples.

What are the two main kinds of kairos rhythms?

Why might it be valuable to identify your church's organizational stage?

What organizational stage do you believe your church is in and why? Are you just entering it, in the middle of it, or coming to the end of it?

How will the next stage on the horizon be different from the stage you are in now?

What ministry seasons do you see in the church right now?

PART 2: KAIROS RHYTHM STRATEGIES

What expectations could the church release for more peace?

What opportunities could the church seize in this time?

What do you anticipate will come next that gives the church hope today?

Of the three kairos rhythm strategies, which is most powerful for your church? Why?

PART 3: CHRONOS RHYTHM STRATEGIES

How would you describe the concept of pacing?

What activities in your church could you put on a better frequency in the five cycles?

In which cycle could your church develop a more healthy flow? Pick one cycle and identify the flow of your church in that cycle.

How would you describe the concept and power of rituals?

What rituals could you establish that would enhance your church?

How would you describe the concept and benefits of oscillation?

How could your church better oscillate between intensity and renewal in one of the five cycles?

CONCLUSION: RHYTHM SOLUTION PROCESS FOR YOUR CHURCH

To what issue or situation in your church would you apply one or more of the six rhythm strategies?

What is the most important idea you have gained from this book?

How will you improve your church with what you have learned? What will you do differently?

What could you do to extend or expand the ideas in this book?

How do you think other church leaders and members will respond to the principles of rhythm?

With whom would you like to share what you've gained from this book?

RHYTHM**OVERVIEW**

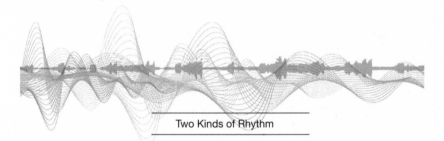

Two Kinds of Rhythm

Kairos	Chronos
Ecclesiastes 3	Genesis 1

ORGANIZATIONAL STAGES

MINISTRY SEASONS

DAY
WEEK
MONTH
QUARTER
YEAR

Six Rhythm Strategies

𝜫 Release expectations.

𝜫 Seize opportunities.

𝜫 Anticipate what's next.

☉ Pace your church.

☉ Build mission-enhancing rituals.

☉ Oscillate intensity and renewal.

NOTES

Introduction: Time: The Forgotten Dimension

1. Pastor Rick Warren led Saddleback Church in a forty-day campaign tied to his book *The Purpose-Driven Life*, which swept the country (Grand Rapids, Mich.: Zondervan, 2002). Since then many churches have done this campaign as well as many others that have imitated his original. See also Rick Warren, *The Purpose-Driven Church: Growth Without Compromising Your Message and Mission* (Grand Rapids, Mich.: Zondervan Publishing, 1995).

2. Gene Getz was a leader in the church renewal movement in the 1970s and '80s. See *The Measure of a Church* (Glendale, Calif.: Regal Books, 1973).

3. Ken Hemphill has had a significant influence in Southern Baptist circles as an author and seminary president. See *The Antioch Effect: 8 Characteristics of Highly Effective Churches* (Nashville: Broadman & Holman, 1994). Mark Dever has influenced the discussion of a healthy church through his books, seminary teaching, and the 9Marks organization. In *Nine Marks of a Healthy Church* (Washington, D.C.: Center for Church Reform, 1998), he examines the need for an outward-looking church that encompasses global mission and local evangelism. Bill Hybels leads Willow Creek Church and the Willow Creek Association, which promoted and modeled the seeker church movement in the 1980s and '90s. See http://www.willowcreek.com.

4. Thom Rainer (2006) says we need to get simple: define one purpose statement (not a purpose, vision, mission, and values statement), then align

everything under that purpose and ruthlessly eliminate everything that doesn't fit. Andy Stanley (2006) focuses on questions to ask to evaluate programs you are considering. He stresses a streamlined approach to ministry with clear targets. Randy Pope (2002) notes that a prevailing church models a dynamic spirit of worship and servanthood, drawing people needing help. According to Reggie McNeal (2009), the Renaissance marked a major shift in our culture and society that paved the way for the Enlightenment and modernity. The reasons the Renaissance found traction (education, technology, wealth), he suggests, are the same as those giving traction to a missional understanding of the church today, and the missional renaissance is no less radical. Church leaders are shifting to be less "religious" and more oriented to "community" and "Kingdom impact." For this to work, we need what he calls a new scorecard that will bring churches and leaders to the same page for knowing what we're doing right. Eric Swanson (2004) states that the church in America today is losing influence when it fails to to deliver a compelling message to those who no longer feel that the church can help them; we need to shift from aiming to be the best church *in* the community to being the best church *for* the community. Robert Lewis (2001) focuses on the need for the church to connect to its surrounding culture by reaching out to the community.

5. *Your Life in Rhythm* presents rhythm strategies for a healthy life. I refute the idea of a "balanced life" as a hurtful concept that creates an idealistic mirage driving guilt and stress. Instead of balance, I suggest "rhythm" as a more powerful metaphor for a God-honoring life. The book offers six rhythm strategies for a better life.

Chapter One: Why Do Church in Rhythm?

1. This point has been made recently by Larry Osborne (2007) in *Contrarian's Guide to Knowing God*, "Seeking Balance: Does God Give a Rip?"

2. In the late 1950s, folksinger Pete Seeger turned this into the song "Turn, Turn, Turn," which in the 1960s was recorded by a number of bands, including, most famously, the Byrds.

3. *Anchor Bible Commentary* (New Haven, Conn.: Yale University Press, 2008, p. 171).

4. Roy Zuck, *Reflecting on Solomon: Selected Studies on the Book of Ecclesiastes* (Grand Rapids, Mich.: Baker, 1994); quote by Castellino is on pages 217 and 222. See also George R. Castellino, "Qohelet and His Wisdom," *Catholic Biblical Quarterly* 30 (January 1968).

5. Russell Foster and Leon Kreitzman, *Rhythms of Life: The Biological Clocks That Control the Daily Lives of Every Living Thing* (New Haven, Conn.: Yale University Press), 2005.

6. Franz Halberg, previous director of the Chronobiology Laboratory at the University of Minneosota, is widely recognized as the father of American chronobiology. He coined the word "circadian." For a list of publications see http://www.msi.umn.edu/~halberg/bib.html.

7. Susan Perry and Jim Dawson, "Clue to Mystery of How Biological Clock Operates on 24-Hour Cycle," *ScienceDaily*, Nov. 29, 2009. http://www.sciencedaily.com/releases/2009/11/091127124849.htm.

Chapter Three: Discerning Your Organizational Stage

1. In Chapter Five of *Your Life in Rhythm* I explore personal life stages.

2. For an application of the sigmoid curve to churches see Kevin Ford, *Transforming Church: Bring Out the Good to Get the Great* (Carol Stream, Ill.: Tyndale, 2007, pp. 161–163). http://www.adizes.com.

3. See Martin Saarinen, *The Life Cycle of a Congregation* (New York: Alban Institute, 1986, p. 5). See also the brief analysis of Michael Dibbert in *Spiritual Leadership, Responsible Management: A Guide for Leaders of the Church*, "Life Cycles: Stages in the Life of a Church," in which he maps four stages: start-up, growth, consolidation, and maturity across church size. His chart on page 167 provides a helpful list of key issues at each stage (Grand Rapids, Mich.: Zondervan Publishing, 1989).

4. George W. Bullard Jr., *Pursuing the Full Kingdom Potential of Your Congregation* (St. Louis, Mo.: Chalice Press, 2005).

5. Floyd Tidsworth in *Life Cycle of a New Congregation* analyzed six substages in the life cycle of a new church plant: discovery, preparation, cultivation, fellowship, mission, and church. In his view new works move from cell group to core group to congregation as organizationally they move from start-up to organization to growth (Nashville: Broadman Press, 1992).

6. See http://www.transformingchurch.com/resourcetoolbox.

Chapter Six: Seize Opportunities

1. See http://3emckinney.com.

Chapter Eight: Pace Your Church

1. See also Hebrews 12:1–4.

2. See http://www.active.com/running/Articles/4-Steps-to-Your-Perfect-Pace.htm.

3. See http://www.active.com/running/Articles/Learn_to_develop_a_sense_of_pace_for_your_running_races.htm.

4. See http://bipolar.about.com/od/treatment/a/990811_pacing.htm.

5. See http://www.franchisebusiness.com.au/c/The-Happiness-Institute/Pacing-your-way-through-life-n858607. For more information see http://www.makingchanges.com.au/

Chapter Nine: Build Mission-Enhancing Rituals

1. Ralph Wiley, "R-Dub Presents Strange But True Sports Rituals." http://espn.go.com/page2/s/wiley/010510.html.

2. See http://dictionary.reference.com/browse/ritual.

3. See http://anthro.palomar.edu/religion/rel_1.htm.

4. William Doherty, "Intentional Marriage: Your Rituals Will Set You Free" (keynote address at Smart Marriages Conference, Denver, 2008). http://www.smartmarriages.com/intentionalmarriage.html.

5. John D. Friesen writes: "Various studies have examined the neurobiological impact of participation in rituals (E. d'Aquili, C. Laughlin, and J. McManus, eds., *The Spectrum of Ritual: Biogenetic Structural Analysis* [New York: Columbia University Press, 1979]). These investigations show that rituals produce positive limbic discharges which lead to warmth and closeness among people. Rituals tend to stimulate both left and right parts of the brain so that the 'two hemispheres of the brain spill over into each other.' The result may be deep emotional experiences, such as a 'shiver down the back.' These experiences have the effect of facilitating personal integration and the feeling of well-being. Rituals tend to combine both digital and analogic levels of information so that logical and verbal methods of communication are combined with nonverbal symbolic methods. Rituals thus hold a level of meaning and significance that words alone cannot capture." Friesen, "Rituals and Family Strength," *Direction Journal,* Spring 1990, *19*(1), 39–48. http://www.directionjournal.org/article/?654.

6. Barbara Biziou provides a brief, accessible introduction to the concept of ritual and shares how to ritualize many common life routines to add value to daily life in *The Joy of Ritual: Spiritual Recipes to Celebrate*

Milestones, Ease Transitions, and Make Every Day Sacred (New York: Cosimo, 1999).

7. "Religious Ritual." In *Anthropology of Religion* (New York: McGraw Hill, 2003). http://highered.mcgraw-hill.com/sites/0072387238/student_view0/chapter7/chapter_summary.html.

8. Barbara H. Fiese and others, "A Review of 50 Years of Research on Naturally Occurring Family Routines and Rituals: Cause for Celebration?" *Journal of Family Psychology*, 2002, *16*(4).

9. Jim Loehr, "The Human Potential: Rewarding Rituals" (*Executive Update Magazine*, June 2003). http://www.asaecenter.org/PublicationsResources/EUArticle.cfm?ItemNumber=11823.

10. Ibid.

11. Lauren Winner, *Mudhouse Sabbath* (Brewster, Mass.: Paraclete Press, 2003). See also Gertrud Mueller Nelson, *To Dance with God: Family Ritual and Community Celebration* (Mahwah, N.J.: Paulist Press, 1986). These authors cover the history, psychology, and spirituality of ritual and then apply that understanding to the Christian year.

12. Andrew Bonar, *The Works of Rev. Robert Murray McCheyne: Complete in One Volume* (New York: Robert Carter, 1874) p. 345.

Chapter Ten: Oscillate Intensity and Renewal

1. Jim Loehr and Tony Schwartz, *The Power of Full Engagement* ((New York: Free Press, 2003), p. 200.

2. Matthew Kelly, *The Rhythm of Life: Living Every Day with Passion and Purpose* (New York: Simon & Schuster/Fireside, 1999), p. 169.

3. Loehr and Schwartz, p. 200.

4. Ibid., p. 12.

5. See http://www.answers.com/topic/oscillation.

6. "The biblical pattern of eating swung between the fast and the feast. Fasting, the abstinence of food, was a sign of repentance and utter dependence on God. Feasting, no less a spiritual discipline, was a sign of the goodness of God. Though most of the Israelites' meals were no doubt simple fare, they knew both seasons of abstinence and the festivals of indulgence (the three most significant being Unleavened Bread, Weeks,

and Booths)." Maxie D. Dunnam, Gordon MacDonald, and Donald W. McCullough, *Mastering Personal Growth* (Sisters, Ore.: Multnomah, 1992, p. 123).

7. See http://www.lib.utexas.edu/etd/d/2008/bournen38875/bournen38875. pdf.

8. See http://www.trifuel.com/training/triathlon-training/what-does-periodization-mean-and-how-does-it-work; http://training.strengthen-gine.com/periodization.shtml; http://www.unm.edu/~lkravitz/Article%20 folder/periodization.html.

9. See http://www.unm.edu/~lkravitz/Article%20folder/periodization.html.

10. See http://training.strengthengine.com/periodization.shtml.

11. Kelly, p. 294.

12. Loehr and Schwartz, p. 12.

13. Mihaly Csikszentmihalyi, *Flow* (New York: HarperCollins, 1990), p. 3.

14. Kay Judge and Maxine Barish-Wreden, "Take Two Vacations and Call Me in the Morning," *Dallas Morning News*, July 1, 2008. See http:// www.relax411online.com/?q=node/108.

15. "Circadian Rhythms Dominate All Life Functions, According to Study" (*ScienceDaily*, June 18, 2007). http://www.sciencedaily.com/releases/ 2007/06/070615075550.htm.

Conclusion: Rhythm Solution Process for Your Church

1. Choon-Leon Seow, "Ecclesiastes," in *The Anchor Bible Commentary* (New York: Doubleday, 1997), p. 171.

2. Larry E. McCall, "Pastoring in the Light of Eternity," *Reformation and Revival Ministries*, Spring 1997, 6(2), 163–172.

3. The Rhythm Solution Process for Churches worksheet is also available as a free download at www.yourlifeinrhythm.com.

4. Henry Hazlitt, *Thinking as a Science* (New York: Dutton, 1916 [1920], p. 17).

REFERENCES

Anchor Bible Commentary. (2008). New Haven, Conn.: Yale University Press.

Balz, Horst, and Schneider, Gerhard. (eds.). (1990–1993). *Exegetical Dictionary of the New Testament.* Grand Rapids, Mich.: Eerdmans.

Bauer, W. (2000). *A Greek-English Lexicon of the New Testament and Other Early Christian Literature,* 3rd. ed. F. W. Danker, ed. W. F. Arndt, F. W. Gingrich, and F. W. Danker, trans. University of Chicago Press: Chicago and London.

Biziou, Barbara. (1999). *The Joy of Ritual: Spiritual Recipes to Celebrate Milestones, East Transitions, and Make Every Day Sacred.* New York: Cosimo.

Bonar, Andrew. (1874). *The Works of Rev. Robert Murray McCheyne: Complete in One Volume.* New York: Robert Carter.

Bourne, Nicholas David. (2008). *Fast Science: A History of Training Theory and Methods for Elite Runners Through 1975* (Ph.D. dissertation). Austin: University of Texas.

Bullard, George W., Jr. (2005). *Pursuing the Full Kingdom Potential of Your Congregation.* St. Louis, Mo.: Chalice Press.

Clinton, J. Robert. (1988). *The Making of a Leader: Recognizing the Lessons and Stages of Leadership Development.* Colorado Springs, Colo.: NAV Press.

Covey, Stephen R. (1989). *Seven Habits of Highly Effective People.* New York: Simon & Schuster.

Csikszentmihalyi, Mihaly. (1990). *Flow.* New York: HarperCollins.

Dever, Mark E. (2009). *Nine Marks of a Healthy Church.* Wheaton, Ill.: Good News Publishers.

Dibbert, Michael. (1989). *Spiritual Leadership, Responsible Management: A Guide for Leaders of the Church.* Grand Rapids, Mich.: Zondervan.

Drucker, Peter. (2008). *Management* (rev. ed.). New York: HarperCollins.

Dunnam, Maxie D., MacDonald, Gordon, and McCullough, Donald W. (1992). *Mastering Personal Growth.* Sisters, Ore.: Multnomah.

Fiese, Barbara, and others. (2002, Dec.). "A Review of 50 Years of Research on Naturally Occurring Family Routines and Rituals: Cause for Celebration?" *Journal of Family Psychology, 16*(4), 381–390.

Ford, Kevin. (2007). *Transforming Church: Bring Out the Good to Get the Great.* Carol Stream, Ill.: Tyndale.

Foster, Russell, and Kreitzman, Leon. (2005). *Rhythms of Life: The Biological Clocks That Control the Daily Lives of Every Living Thing.* New Haven, Conn.: Yale University Press.

Frankel, Christopher, and Kravitz, Len. (2000). "Periodization: Latest Studies and Practical Applications." *IDEA Personal Trainer, 11*(1), 15–16.

Friesen, John D. (1990, spring). "Rituals and Family Strength." *Direction Journal, 19*(1).

Getz, Gene. (1974). *Sharpening the Focus of the Church.* Chicago: Moody Press.

Handy, Charles. (1995). *The Age of Paradox.* Cambridge, Mass.: Harvard University Business Press.

Haire, Mason. (1959). *Modern Organization Theory.* New York: Wiley.

Hazlitt, Henry. (1920 [1916]). *Thinking as a Science.* New York: Dutton.

Hemphill, Kenneth. (1994). *The Antioch Effect: 8 Characteristics of Highly Effective Churches.* Nashville: Broadman & Holman.

Ireton, Kimberlee Conway. (2008). *The Circle of Seasons: Meeting God in the Church Year.* Downers Grove, Ill.: IVP Books.

Judge, Kay, and Barish-Wreden, Maxine. (2008, July 1). "Take Two Vacations and Call Me in the Morning." *Dallas Morning News.*

Kelly, Matthew. (1999). *The Rhythm of Life: Living Every Day with Passion and Purpose.* New York: Simon & Schuster.

Kittel, Gerhard, and Friedrich, Gerhard. (1964–1976). *Theological Dictionary of the New Testament.* 10 vols. Grand Rapids, Mich.: Eerdmans.

Kotter, Jon. (1996). *Leading Change.* Cambridge, Mass.: Harvard University Business Press.

Kübler-Ross, E. (1969). *On Death and Dying*. New York: Routledge.

Lencioni, Patrick. (2004). *Death by Meeting*. New York: Wiley.

Lewis, Robert. (2001). *The Church of Irresistible Influence*. Grand Rapids, Mich.: Zondervan.

Loehr, Jim, and Schwartz, Tony. (2003). *The Power of Full Engagement*. New York: Free Press.

Mancini, Will. (2008). *Church Unique: How Missional Leaders Cast Vision, Capture Culture, and Create Movement*. San Francisco: Jossey-Bass.

McCall, Larry E. (1997, spring). "Pastoring in the Light of Eternity." *Reformation and Revival Ministries*, 6(2), 163–172.

McNeal, Reggie. (2009). *Missional Renaissance: Changing the Scorecard for the Church*. San Francisco: Jossey-Bass.

Miller, Bruce. (2009). *Your Life in Rhythm*. Carol Stream, Ill.: Tyndale.

Nelson, Gertrud Mueller. (1986). *To Dance with God: Family Ritual and Community Celebration*. Mahwah, N.J.: Paulist Press.

Osborne, Larry. (2006). *The Unity Factor: Developing a Healthy Leadership Team*, 4th ed. Vista, Calif.: Owl's Nest.

Osborne, Larry. (2007). "Seeking Balance: Does God Give a Rip?" In *Contrarian's Guide to Knowing God*. New York: WaterBrook Multnomah Publishing Group, a division of Random House.

Osborne, Larry. (2010). *Sticky Teams: Keeping Your Leadership Team and Staff on the Same Page*. Grand Rapids, Mich.: Zondervan.

Perry, Susan, and Dawson, Jim. (1988). *Secrets Our Body Clocks Reveal: How to Tune Into Your Body's Rhythms to Perform at Your Peak Day or Night*. New York: Rawson Associates.

Peterson, Eugene H. (2002). *The Message: The Bible in Contemporary Language*. Colorado Springs, Colo.: NavPress.

Pope, R. M. (1910–1911). "Studies in Pauline Vocabulary: Redeeming the Time." *Expository Times*, 22, 552–554.

Pope, Randy. (2002). *The Prevailing Church: An Alternative Approach to Ministry*. Chicago: Moody Press.

Rainer, Thom, and Geiger, Eric. (2006). *Simple Church: Returning to God's Process for Making Disciples*. Nashville: Broadman & Holman.

Saarinen, Martin. (1986). *The Life Cycle of a Congregation*. New York: The Alban Institute.

Schwarz, Christian A. (1996). *Natural Church Development: A Guide to Eight Essential Qualities of Healthy Churches*. Saint Charles, Ill.: ChurchSmart Resources.

Sheehy, Gail. (1974). *Passages*. New York: Ballantine Books.

Sheehy, Gail. (1996). *New Passages: Mapping Your Life Across Time*. New York: Ballantine Books.

Simon, Judith Sharken. (2001). *The Five Life Stages of Nonprofit Organizations: Where You Are, Where You're Going, and What to Expect When You Get There*. Saint Paul, Minn.: Wilder Foundation.

Stanley, Andy, Jones, Lane, and Joiner, Reggie. (2006). *Seven Practices of Effective Ministry*. Sisters, Ore.: Multnomah.

Swanson, Eric, and Rusaw, Rick. (2004). *The Externally Focused Church*. Loveland, Colo.: Group Publishing.

Tidsworth, Floyd. (1992). *Life Cycle of a New Congregation*. Nashville: Broadman Press.

Warren, Rick. (1990). *The Purpose-Driven Church: Growth Without Compromising Your Message and Mission*. Grand Rapids, Mich.: Zondervan.

Warren, Rick. (2002). *The Purpose-Driven Life*. Grand Rapids, Mich.: Zondervan.

Winner, Lauren. (2003). *Mudhouse Sabbath*. Brewster, Mass.: Paraclete Press.

Zuck, Roy. (1994). *Reflecting with Solomon: Selected Studies on the Book of Ecclesiastes*. Grand Rapids, Mich.: Baker Book House.

THE**AUTHOR**

B ruce B. Miller has been married to Tamara since 1983 and is father to five children: Bart, Jimmy, David, Melanie, and Ben. His passions are developing leaders and communicating ideas for the multiplication of Christ's church. He helped found the Center for Church Based Training (www.ccbt.org), where he served as chairman of the board for many years. He did doctoral work in the history of ideas at the University of Texas, Dallas, with a focus in philosophical hermeneutics. In 1997, with a great team, Bruce planted McKinney Fellowship Bible Church which, because of an expanded vision, is now Christ Fellowship (www.christfellowshiphome.com) in McKinney, Texas, where he now serves as senior pastor. Previously he taught theology in a seminary and served as a staff pastor with Gene Getz, as well as serving as pastor of a small church plant in north Texas. He has written *The Leadership Baton* with Jeff Jones and Rowland Forman, and *Your Life in Rhythm* (www.yourlifeinrhythm.com), the forerunner to *Your Church in Rhythm*. He offers church and business leaders seminars and workshops based on the rhythm concepts as well as other topics. Bruce blogs at http://www.christfellowshiphome.com/bruces-blog; Facebook: facebook.com/BruceMillerAuthor; Twitter: twitter.com/bruce_b_miller.

INDEX

Page references followed by *fig* indicate an illustrated figure.

Building projects, 98–99
Bullard, Rev. George, 35, 36

C

Canadian Baptist Theological College, 76
Capital campaign: as ministry season marker, 54; releasing expectations during, 66–67; seizing opportunities during, 82–83
Case studies: A Church on Its Last Legs, 153; A Current Pastor Has a Large New Vision, 55–56; Dramatic Drop in Income and a Lawsuit, xxvi–xxvii; Internal Attack by a Top Leader, 87–88; Major Culture Shift with New Pastor, 25–26; Newly Planted Church in Crisis, 137–138; Pastor Resigns and Executive Pastor Takes Over, 119–120; Prelaunch a Church Plant, 69–70; Relocation and Name Change, 104–105; A Stagnant Church Is Leaderless Between Pastors, 42
Change: being alert for signals on coming, 94–95; crisis over, 40, 67; how conversations can lead to, 84–85; seizing opportunities during, 83; of staff relationships during growth stage, 63–64. *See also* Anticipating what's next
Change-management process, 50
Charter school, 86
Chase Oaks Church (Texas), 59, 81
Choon-Leong Seow, 156
Christ Fellowship, 103
Christmas: as annual chronos cycle, 47; Christmas Eve services, 132;

kairos/chronos rhythms of, 20, 47
Chronobiologic paradigm of science, 9
Chronobiology: natural rhythms studied by, 9; on *zeitgebers* (time givers) cues, 11
Chronos cycles: biblical narratives on, 8–9; comparing kairos seasons to listed, 24–25; created by God, 4, 20; experienced as clock and calendar time, 18–19, 22–25; oscillation applied to all five, 146–152; power of living in rhythm through flow of, 152; predictable and universal nature of, 47–48; Rhythm Solution Process for maximizing, 159–162; theological perspective on, 20–21; understanding cyclical rhythms of, 18; understanding difference between kairos and, 18–20
Chronos rhythm strategies: building mission-enhancing rituals, 123–138; oscillating intensity and renewal, 139–154; pacing your church, 109–122
Chronos rhythms: exercise on describing, 26; harmony of all five, 23*fig*; as important part of rhythm approach, 23–25; kairos rhythms complemented by, 104; lunar (monthly), 21, 23; orbital (annual), 21, 23; rotational (daily), 21, 23; Sabbath (weekly), 21, 23; seasonal (quarterly), 21, 23. *See also* Kairos rhythms; Rhythm approach
Church annual cycle: creating oscillation by charting, 146–147;

Mary and Martha, 142
Matthew 11:28-30, 142
Matthew 13:18-23, 75
Matthew 14:23, 143
Matthew 25:21-23, 157
Maturity stage: anticipating what's
  next during, 97; church during,
  38; organizational, 32; releasing
  expectations during, 63–64;
  seizing opportunities during, 81
M'Cheyne, Robert Murray, 134
The Message (Peterson), 142
Miller, Ben, 124
Miller, David, 124
Miller, Melanie, 17, 124
Miller, Norm, 86–87
Ministry: how an artificial idealism
  harms a, 3–4; rhythm approach
  for balanced, 12–13. *See also*
  Rhythm approach
Ministry patterns, 11–12
Ministry season markers: building
  projects, 98–99; capital campaign,
  54, 66–67, 82–83; charter school,
  86; church plant, 84; church-
  family conversations as, 53;
  citywide evangelism, 86–87;
  community and the pastor
  rhythms, 68–69; conversations
  leading to change, 84–85; crisis,
  40, 52, 67, 83; false teaching, 99;
  grief as, 49–50, 68; pastoral
  transition, 67, 83; sexual
  accusation, 100; sharing in order
  to discern, 53–54
Ministry seasons: anticipating what's
  next during, 98–104;
  commonsense markers of,
  53–54; crisis as triggering a, 52;

A Current Pastor Has a Large
  New Vision case study on, 55–56;
  description of, 28; distinguishing
  organizational stages from, 46–48;
  "ending" category of, 51–52;
  exercise on identifying your
  church's, 56; grief cycle of, 49–50,
  68; identified by significant
  experiences, 48; "interim," 52;
  recognizing common, 48–53;
  releasing expectations during,
  65–69; restructuring category of,
  52; seizing opportunities during,
  82–87; "starting" category of,
  50–51; story of our church's,
  100–104
Mission-enhancing rituals: exercise
  on, 138; longer cycles and
  traditions of, 129–133; Newly
  Planted Church in Crisis case
  study on, 137–138; shorter cycles
  habits of, 133–137. *See also*
  Rituals
Modern Organization Theory
  (Haire), 30
Moltke, Helmuth von, 77
Monastic community rituals,
  133–134
Mordecai, 73
Moses, 33–34, 156
Mother's Day Out program, 47–48,
  86, 100

N

Natural Church Development
  (Schwarz), 80
Nehemiah, 34
New Hope Church (Hawaii), 134
New Passages (Sheehy), 29